Come Rain or Come Shine

A White Parent's Guide to Adopting
and Parenting Black Children

Rachel Garlinghouse

ISBN: 1478310863

ISBN 13: 9781478310860

Library of Congress Control Number: 2012913614
CreateSpace, North Charleston, South Carolina

Acknowledgements

I am thankful to the many individuals who have made my lifelong dream to publish a book come true.

To my husband who stepped out in faith and traveled the adoption path with me.

To my three beautiful children, Miss E, Baby E, and Baby I: I am incredibly honored to have the privilege of being your mom. You bless me in indescribable ways.

To my father who told me to write every day; you're the best, Dad!

To my mother who encouraged my love of reading, writing, and creating, and who didn't fill my days with scheduled activities but instead made me go outside and let me read until midnight.

To the rest of my family, including my husband's family and my siblings, who give me encouragement and honesty.

To my children's birth families for giving their children life and for being a continual blessing to our family. We love you dearly and pray this book reflects our adoration for you.

To the Adoptive Mamas of the Metro, my village, for their wisdom, insight, and support.

To Amy Stockwell Mercer and Amy Ford, who mentored me through the publishing process.

To the Niles family, the Gafford family, and my cousins Bob and Adrian Johnson, who were the first people to encourage and support us in adopting transracially.

To Shelley Newman, Linda Jaworski-Moiles, and Jackie Bruns, for always taking my phone calls to address my adoption panic moments.

To Lindsay, Mary, Dawn, Julie, April, Jim, Tracy, and Susan: for bringing my dream to adopt to fruition.

To Mike and Kay Paulsen for supporting us in our open adoptions and for opening their home to us time and time again. We love you dearly!

To Jazmine Sanders, my girls' mentor, for the many hours she spent playing with the girls so I could write and proof this book.

To my cover and author photographer, Jill Heupel of Jill Heupel Photography in Edwardsville, IL and graphic designer Natalie Smith, family friend, for making this book beautiful.

To the many authors who granted me permission to quote their brilliant findings and experiences. Thank you for your encouragement and wisdom.

Above all, I'm most thankful to God, that You turned my pain into joy, my darkness into light, and my dreams into reality. May this book and all I do in my life bring honor and glory to You.

Praise for Come Rain or Come Shine

*"This highly readable book is vital for any prospective
or current adoptive parent, especially those considering
transracial adoption. From the first thoughts of 'Am I right
for this?' through dealing with friends and family, naming or
re-naming the child, issues of attachment, confronting racism,
even how to care for the hair and skin of a child from a different
race, Garlinghouse delivers a message of empowerment and
even joy, sensitively laced with her personal journey as the
white mother of two African-American girls. She beautifully
conveys the richness of adoption, if we, as Garlinghouse says,
'Create the world you want your children to behold.'"*

~J.S. PICARIELLO, ADOPTEE AND CO-AUTHOR OF JESSICA LOST:
A STORY OF BIRTH, ADOPTION & THE MEANING OF MOTHERHOOD

*"As a transracial adoptive mother of two, I found myself
nodding at every word Rachel writes, as I saw our own
adoption experience reflected in every chapter. She has
condensed in a few pages just about everything you need
to know as a prospective transracial adoptive parent and
everything you want to keep in mind if you are already
into the journey. Her list of resources at the end of every
chapter will be invaluable to anyone who is thinking about
transracial adoption or already down the path, no matter at
what stage. A book definitely worth owning so you can refer
back to over and over again."*

~GABY JOHNSON, ADOPTIVE MOTHER

"This is an incredible amount of information that most adoptive parents would find extremely helpful and forthcoming. I like Rachel's no-nonsense approach and appreciate the basic truths and challenges that she delivers."

~REBEKAH PINCHBACK, ADOPTIVE MOTHER AND ADOPTION BLOGGER (*HEART CRIES*)

"With the clarity of a teacher and the compassion of a parent, Rachel Garlinghouse provides a valuable roadmap for navigating the complexities of transracial adoption. Her slim book is bursting with practical advice, useful examples, and a reservoir of resources that make Come Rain or Come Shine a treasure trove for new adoptive parents."

~JANA WOLFF, ADOPTIVE MOTHER AND AUTHOR OF *SECRET THOUGHTS OF AN ADOPTIVE MOTHER*

"Rachel combines a wealth of facts with real-life stories to make a very informative adoption resource. She shares her extensive knowledge from years of research and personal experience with trans-racial adoption."

~BRIAN AND BETH HUFF, ADOPTIVE PARENTS

"Rachel's first-hand knowledge of adoption from a parent's point of view gives her an empathetic and unique perspective, especially on the topics of open and transracial adoption. The simple and concise format makes it easy to navigate the many concerns and questions that accompany these issues.

This book is especially helpful because Rachel also lists several other resources to help dive further into each topic. This book is a wonderful tool for any couple considering adoption."

~MARY CHAPMAN, FORMER ADOPTION
MANAGER FOR THE LIGHT HOUSE

"Mrs. Garlinghouse's book is a guide to those beginning the adoption process, those who have adopted, and is also a wonderful resource to professionals working with adopted children and their families. Transracially adopted children have unique challenges and life experiences that Mrs. Garlinghouse's book addresses with research, real life examples, humor, and class. This book accurately depicts the 'conspicuous' nature of a transracial family, as well as the joys and trials associated with parenting a child of another race. From reading this book, I have left with ideas to use with my own daughter, as well as with students I work with on a daily basis."

~JENNA TATE, ELEMENTARY SCHOOL COUNSELOR
AND ADOPTIVE MOTHER

Table of Contents

Prologue

*"By wisdom a house is built,
and through understanding it is established;
through knowledge its rooms are filled
with rare and beautiful treasures."*

~Proverbs 24:3-4

I'm no one special.

I'm not an adoption attorney, counselor, or social worker. I'm not a birth parent. I'm not an adoptee. My mom, dad, and siblings—all are my biological relatives.

I'm just a mom who opened her mind to the possibility of adoption, and then transracial adoption, and then I awoke to the bizarre, bittersweet, and beautiful world called transracial adoptive parenting.

So, why should you read this book?

Because I'm ordinary. I'm much like each of you thumbing through these pages—someone who, one day, recognized that adoption might be the way to build my family. I'm the woman sitting next to you who faced a difficult diagnosis and realized that adoption was the path to parenthood. I'm someone who went through the ups and downs of a home study process. I sat down one day and thought, *Could we adopt transracially?* I waited for my first baby—fourteen months of excruciating, soul-searching, endless waiting. I became a mom—now three times—through transracial adoption. I am still learning to navigate open adoption. I'm figuring out what it means to be a Black-White/White-Black family. I'm learning to care for Black hair, share adoption with my children, and explain the adoption phenomenon to the oh-so-curious public that asks never-ending questions. Why couldn't I have my "own" children? Why didn't my girls' birth parents "want" them? Have I heard that so-and-so celebrity is adopting? How cool is that? You get the picture. Transracial adoptive parenting is a unique and mind-boggling experience, one you do not have to navigate alone.

When Steve and I began our adoption journey, our adoption education was miniscule at best. Our adoption agency provided us with little how-to. Instead they asked for paperwork and money and decisions. The journey was confusing and exhilarating—a blur of moments and a whirlwind of emotions. Our profile was shown approximately fifteen times to expectant parents. Yet each time, another family was chosen or we learned that though the expectant parents really liked us, they had decided to parent their baby.

For the first year of waiting for baby number one, we were only open to a healthy White baby, like most White parents waiting to adopt domestically. We chose that route because it seemed the most natural. We hadn't given transracial adoption much thought at that point, and our agency didn't prompt us to consider adopting a child of any race. But after a year we asked ourselves why we weren't we open to it, and both of us felt our hearts stir a bit. It was a bizarre, uncomfortable, and interesting season in our adoption journey.

So our true adoption education began. We met with a new transracial adoptive family to ask questions we didn't dare venture to ask our agency—the questions you think of while you're lying in bed, restless with adoption stress. *Can we love a child who doesn't match us racially? Will the child grow up to hate us because everyone under the sun reminds the child that his or her parents are—gasp—White?*

We read stacks of adoption books, engaged in heated discussions on online adoption forums, and talked—a lot. In fact, for about four months, we talked about transracial adoption every single evening—why we weren't open to it, why we should be, what our fears were, and what our experiences were with people of other races. We knew that our decision could alter our lives dramatically and forever, and we weren't going to enter into transracial adoption with blinders on.

After our marathon months of conversations and much reflection, we concluded that, yes, we could be great parents to a child of any race. We told our social worker of our decision, figuring that our adoption education had come to a close and that we were ready to parent. *Let's move on.*

The moment our first baby arrived, we realized that there was so much more to this adoption thing than just bringing home a child and living happily ever after. We had brought home a *Black* child. Every time we walked into a store or a restaurant, the stares, questions, and comments we encountered reminded us that our family was under a spotlight. People wondered, asked, and assumed; in essence, they wanted answers, answers we didn't have. We weren't the couple in the room with the darling newborn—swaddled in a pink blanket—sleeping in her stroller. We were the couple with the brown-skinned, afro-headed, coffee-colored-eyes, darling newborn. The reality is that despite popular pronouncements, the world is not colorblind, prejudice didn't evaporate after the civil rights movement, and being White still comes with many privileges that brown-skinned individuals do not have.

What I want you to know is that successful transracial adoptive parenting is possible, but you have to work at it—tirelessly—by arming yourself with resources and reaching out for help. There truly never is a better time than the present. It's time to step up to the proverbial plate and prepare yourself and your family for the reality of transracial, adoptive family life—with all of its possibilities, opportunities, hardships, and triumphs.

It's been over four years since my family took on the transracial label. I've read hundreds of adoption books, articles, and blog entries, and I've written several adoption articles and blog entries myself, all from the perspective of the transracial-adoptive parenting trenches. I've consulted with dozens of prospective adoptive parents, answering their questions, pointing them to resources, and encouraging them. I have walked the adoption journey with a birth mother — from her pregnancy to delivery to placement, and now, post-placement — and through all the highs and lows each season entailed. My communication with educators, counselors, social workers, adoptees, and birth parents has furthered my adoption education. Searching, learning, and evolving never stops. Many transracial adoptive parents will do whatever it takes to ensure their child's success, instill a strong sense of self-worth, and affirm and foster racial identity.

Getting started, or finding the motivation to continue the learning process, can be daunting. I assure you that you are surrounded by possibilities, encouragement, and resources, and I'm here to point you to those places and people who can help enrich your transracial adoption and parenting journey.

Are you ready?

CHAPTER ONE

Choosing Transracial Adoption: Getting Started

*"Those who cannot change their minds cannot
change anything."*

~George Bernard Shaw

My journey to adoption began in a hospital room. I was lying in a bed in the fetal position, my tiny frame curled uncomfortably, trying to accommodate the multiple tubes and monitors protruding from my body. A designated educator, perched in a green vinyl chair, was droning on about needles and insulin and counting carbohydrates. I was coming back from the dead, literally, and I was exhausted. With the little energy I had left, I generated anger and hopelessness. My husband, dedicated and patient, was sitting by my bedside, listening carefully to the educator's words.

Catching my eye, the educator asked, "Do you two plan to have children?"

With just one question, she had my immediate and full attention. Steve and I answered "yes," simultaneously and without hesitation.

"You still can, you know," she said gently, realizing that for the first time since I had been in the hospital, she was offering me some good news. She then began to explain what pregnancy with type 1 diabetes might look like.

And in that moment, a single word popped into my mind, and I refused to let it go.

Adoption.

Who Adopts—and Why?

Many people consider adopting. The idea initially seems exotic, noble, exhilarating. Maybe you were one of those people, thinking that maybe one day you would adopt a child or two. Like many, you may have told yourself something like this: *I'll have a few kids of my own first.* Then, *if my family still feels incomplete, I'll adopt. Adoption – doesn't it seem so incredible?*

Most commonly, adoption is chosen as the option for building families because a person or couple cannot have a child biologically. Some couples have one biological child, only to face secondary infertility when they attempt to conceive again. Perhaps medical assistance, such as IVF, has failed. Surrogacy may not be an option due to moral objections or cost.

Others, such as those in my circumstance, face a difficult diagnosis that makes pregnancy dangerous or potentially deadly for the mother or unborn child. Either or both prospective parents could be carriers of a disease or disorder that might possibly pass on to any biological children.

Others adopt simply out of the desire to do so. Some have family members or friends who were adopted, which prompt them to consider adoption for their own families. Others wish to adopt a child from a specific country, of a specific race, a sibling pair or group, or a child with special needs. Some are single and wish to adopt rather than wait for the perfect partner to come along and then have a child.

No matter the journey that brings one to consider adoption, there seems to be a common denominator: change. For some, the change might be positive, but for many prospective adoptive parents, it was unwelcome and unplanned—such as infertility, disease, divorce, death, or diagnosis. Each of these brings about its own consequences and complications.

Some enter into adoption knowing they will adopt transracially while others come to the conclusion that transracial adoption is right for them later on in their adoption journeys. The first step is an adoption decision, and the next step is to prepare for transracial adoptive parenthood.

Loss and Grief

It's important that those who wish to adopt proceed with their plans only after they have grieved and dealt with the loss in their lives. Mary Watkins and Susan Fisher, authors of *Talking With Young Children About Adoption*, write, "Adoptive parents who have not come to terms with their own infertility and who feel, as a result, insecure, inferior, and defective may be rejecting, overprotective, overindulgent, or less deeply attached to their adopted child and thus may contribute to his emotional problems" (45).

Transracial adoption is a life-altering decision, one that demands attention and education. Allowing past experiences to cloud your vision and hinder your learning experience will not benefit your child. Furthermore, your child may come with physical, psychological, emotional, or social needs that you will need to be fully prepared to deal with. With the unique and new circumstances adoption invites into a person's life, it's practical to begin the journey with a clean slate.

Sherrie Eldridge shares in her book *Twenty Things Adopted Kids Wish Their Adoptive Parents Knew*: "Once you have successfully grieved the losses in your own life, you will be a 'safe person' to your child—one to whom she is free to express any emotion without fear of condemnation or judgment. You will provide a place brimming with welcoming acceptance, one that encourages conversation about your child's feelings surrounding adoption" (27).

Losses that parents pursuing adoption might experience, according to Patricia Irwin Johnston, author of *Adoption is a Family Affair: What Relatives and Friends Must Know!*, include the loss of blending their own genetics with another's to "create a unique human being who is the ultimate expression of the love they share," the loss "of the opportunity to become pregnant or make someone pregnant" while also experiencing "the physical and emotional benefit and expectations our culture has taught us to desire and expect from pregnancy and birth," the loss of "extending the family blood line," and the loss of "control over privacy in planning a family" (18-19).

Seeking assistance for coping with loss is recommended. Seeing a professional counselor, joining a support group (in person or online), or researching your specific struggle can be helpful. Personally, I have found exercising, dietary changes, and blogging to be cathartic.

The grief process has no set timeframe or deadline; however, it's crucial that you fully cope with whatever circumstances led you to adoption, positive and negative. Once you arrive at the acceptance stage, you will be prepared to decide if adoption truly is the best choice for you.

Your loss will always be a part of your life, whether you adopt or not, and it makes you who you are. Even after you grieve a loss, it can creep back on you as you move forward with your life, and you may need to revisit whatever works to restore you. This commonly happens with adoptive families — especially transracial adoptive families, who are constantly reminded that they are an *adoptive* family by the comments and questions they face from family, friends, and the general public. Some finally receive a child — after months or years of waiting — only to feel overwhelmed with sadness as reminders of past loss come up. Extended and intrusive feelings, as elaborated on in chapter 3, can be signs of Post-Adoption Depression.

If you are currently facing a major change in your life, be it losing a job or starting a new job, a divorce, the death of a close family member or friend, a new diagnosis, or a new marriage, allow yourself time for adjustment, healing, and growth before pursuing an adoption.

Adoptive Parents Are Not...

The adoption community is plagued by preconceived notions of what adoption should be, what it is, and what it isn't. Adoption is its own world: confusing, bittersweet, and interesting. Mainly, adoption is misunderstood.

Prospective adoptive parents need to enter into adoption knowing who they are and who they aren't. When you establish your identity as an adoptive parent, you will be better prepared to face challenges.

- *Adoptive parents are not saviors.* Yes, many children who are adopted were previously in dire and dangerous circumstances. Some children languish in orphanages for months or even years. Some children come from the domestic foster care system, where they were perhaps bounced from house to house after being removed from their biological family. Other children were born into less-than-ideal circumstances such as extraordinary poverty or abuse. But keep in mind that some children have been relinquished to an adoptive family by biological parents who felt they were not able to parent at that time, and that this choice was made out of love and selflessness. Sadly, some children become available for adoption because their biological parents were coerced into relinquishing their rights, or in some cases, the children were stolen or sold from their biological families. The point is, children come into adoption through a variety of circumstances.

    In the case of transracial adoption, it's clearly evident that the child was adopted, and therefore, even more assumptions are made about his or her past. Watch any "save these poor, helpless children" commercials prompting you to donate just $1 a day, and you'll notice that the children featured are almost always brown-skinned.

Adoptive parents will face the "savior" comment many times in one form or another. "There are so many children who need good homes." Or, "Your child is so lucky to have you as her parents." It is dangerous to the self-worth of the child for parents to accept this "compliment" as it puts the child in a less-than position and puts the adoptive parents on a pedestal. In a society where the darker the person's skin, the less privilege (and more discrimination) he or she encounters, it's crucial that adoptive parents do not allow further disadvantages, such as the "savior" mentality, to plague their children's lives.

- *Adoptive parents are not child-stealers.* No doubt, unethical adoptions occur, but the vast majority of adoptive parents I have encountered want a "clean" adoption, one that is ethical.

  Particularly in the case of transracial adoption, adoptive parents will face scrutiny from both individuals of their own race and of the child's race. In some cultures and geographic locations and to people of older generations, transracial adoption is unacceptable, taboo, or simply strange. I recall being approached by an older African American man who asked if the child beside me was my daughter. I said yes, and his reply was, "Really?" I told him yes, she really was my daughter following that with the fact that she was adopted. He then said, "I'm older, mind you, so I haven't really seen this. May I ask, why didn't you adopt one of your own kind?" The man's age and his racial upbringing contributed to his view of my family.

  Transracial adoptive parents will inevitably face the judgments of others, but it's important for them to establish from the get-go that they are not child-stealers just because their child has a different racial background. In many adoption cases, the child was voluntarily relinquished for adoption because the biological parents felt it was the best decision for the child. In some cases, the biological parents chose the adoptive family, and the family's race wasn't enough of an issue for the biological parents to reject the adoptive family. Respecting the biological parents' decision to place the child, which happened to be transracially, is something that adoptive parents need to convey both to the public and to the adopted child.

- *Adoptive parents are often not wealthy.* One of the questions I am frequently asked is, "Isn't adoption really expensive?" The answer is that adoption *can* be expensive. However, some adoptions are free of cost, or nearly free, such as domestic foster care adoption. Furthermore, many adoptive parents have already spent much of what they had on infertility treatments or medical bills related to a diagnosis. Many of the adoptive families I speak with work creatively and diligently to raise funds for their adoption costs. Some take out loans, accept donations, and host fundraisers. After the child arrives, the adoptive family must then take on traditional child-rearing expenses such as food, clothing, medical insurance, and child care — all of which are, as all parents know, quite costly.

  Transracial adoption, in particular, often has the public questioning the intentions of the adoptive parents. I have been asked why White people feel the need to adopt Black children. Are White parents trying to save Black children? Are we swooping in to offer the child a greater future, full of Disney vacations and Pottery Barn bedroom décor, something that the stereotypical Black family cannot?

  Adoptive parents may wish to respond to the wealth-question by sharing that people from many different economic backgrounds adopt. You may also point those who question the cost of adoption toward a local agency. The specifics of how much your adoption cost is personal information that isn't required to be shared. Though much of the adoption process is invasive by nature, adoptive families can rightfully choose not to disclose financial information to family members, friends, and strangers.

- *Adoptive parents are not a replacement for the child's biological parents.* Adoptees will always have two sets of parents: one by birth and one by adoption. No matter the circumstances of how the child came to be adopted, the fact is that the child was conceived by his or her birth parents and shares their genes and other parts of them, such as some preferences and some personality characteristics.

    The public tends to dismiss the biological parents due to stereotypes. I have been asked on numerous occasions if my children's birth parents were young or on drugs. Parents who adopt transracially will find that stereotypes regarding the child's race, such as that Black people are typically poor or that many use drugs or are criminals, will shape how the adoptive parents and the adoptee are perceived by the public.

    Your child's biological parents will always be the child's biological parents and will forever be significant part of your child, whether you have an open adoption or not. It's essential that adoptive parents, much like in a divorced-couple situation, always seek to defuse any negative discussions or comments regarding "the other" in the situation. Specific details of the child's adoption story that are difficult (such as a history of abuse, conception from rape, drug use, etc.) should be shared at the right time and in the right way with the child, but not with just anyone who asks.

    Because your child will be adopted transracially, it will be clearly evident that the child has another set of parents. You will be reminded often that your child is adopted, and you will be asked questions about the child's birth (first) parents. Adoptive families should work to resolve any jealousy or anger issues they have surrounding the child's biological parents, because the adoptive parent's attitudes toward the birth parents will be evident to the child, most importantly, and to anyone who asks about the child's birth parents.

Is Transracial Adoption Right for Your Family?

Transracial adoption may not be the best choice for your family if…

- You live in a racist area and cannot move at this time.

- You live in an overwhelmingly White community and cannot move at this time.

- You wish to adopt transracially because your agency or attorney has a reduced fee for transracial adoption or because you can adopt more quickly if the child is a minority.

- Your partner doesn't wish to pursue transracial adoption.

- You do not intend to adopt more than one child transracially or you do not have any other minority or multi-racial children currently in your home or in your close circle of friends or relatives.

- You intend to adopt and "move on," dismissing any further adoption discussion.

- You aren't interested in learning more about adoption, your child's racial culture, or transracial adoption.

- Your extended family member(s) and friends are strongly against transracial adoption, and you do not intend to choose your child over your family or friends by breaking off communication, if necessary, with those who oppose your decision.

- You aren't a person who faces confrontation when necessary.

- You believe that love conquers all problems and that love is all your family needs to be a successful transracial adoptive family.

You might be a good candidate for transracial adoption if...

- You live in a diverse community that is accepting of transracial adoption.

- Your partner is interested in transracial adoption and is committed to the process.

- You intend to adopt more than one minority child.

- You already have minority or multi-racial children in your home.

- You intend to allow adoption, race, and transracial adoption to be an ongoing and open topics of conversation in your home.

- You are dedicated to learning about and including your child's racial culture as a part of your daily lives.

- You are willing, if necessary, to disconnect from prejudiced family members and friends.

- You face confrontation when necessary.

- You are determined to face transracial parenthood with love *and* education.

Questions from the Trenches

I have determined that adoption is the only way to build our family, yet I can't help but wonder if we should try just one more round of IVF. Is it OK to do IVF while simultaneously beginning our adoption process?

This is a personal decision; however, your adoption agency or attorney might require that you not pursue infertility treatments while working on an adoption process. The thought is that you need to be fully committed to adopting before proceeding with an adoption. Furthermore, many agencies are concerned that you will pull out of the adoption process should you become pregnant after you are matched with a child, severing your commitment to the child (and, potentially, the child's biological parents).

Some prospective adoptive parents secretly pursue infertility treatments while adopting, despite their adoption agency's preferences or rules. I recommend being completely honest with your adoption agency. It is easy for prospective adoptive parents to become frustrated with their agency because it seems to hold the key to parenthood and is, as a rule, intrusively and intimately involved in the prospective adoptive parents' lives. However, this is the nature of the adoption process, and being dishonest can be harmful to all involved.

If you wish to pursue both infertility treatments and an adoption at the same time, choose an agency that accepts this. However, I suggest that you do not enter into adoption, and especially transracial adoption, half-heartedly. It is crucial that adoptive parents pursue loss resolution before, during, and after an adoption takes place. It is not fair to the transracially adopted, brown-skinned child to be seen by his or her White parents as second-best to a White child. Many adoptive parents might vow not to let the child ever know their true feelings, but children are amazingly perceptive and could quite possibly pick up on conversations, facial expressions, and gossip that tells him or her that Mommy or Daddy really preferred a White, biological child first and foremost. Obviously, this could be devastating for the child.

As we share our adoption decision with family and friends, we keep facing the statement, "Oh! A child will be so lucky to have you as parents! There are so many children who need good homes." While we are happy to receive such a warm response, we're concerned that once our child arrives, he or she will be perceived as a victim or a charity case, not our son or daughter.

You are right to assume that the comment is meant to be welcoming, not harmful; however, when it is made in front of your child, it *is* harmful. The statement assumes that the child is better off because of you and that he or she is the lucky one. The assumption that adoptive-parent-as-a-savior is common.

A simple, "We will be the lucky ones!" puts the focus on the fact that you are adopting because you want to be parents, not because you are searching for a child to "save" from whatever stereotypical circumstances the family member or friend believes the child must come from.

Furthermore, their exclamation gives you an opportunity to state the truth about adopting children of color. Many people aren't open to it (domestically or internationally) which is one reason there aren't enough adoptive homes for minority kids. But one never knows the power of an honest and open education. One woman who decided to adopt from Ethiopia chose to take her father with her as her travel companion. After seeing some harsh realities, my friend's father chose to adopt a child himself. Had my friend not offered to share the journey with her father, she wouldn't have a newly adopted brother.

Prospective adoptive parents walk a fine line between educating others in a way that speaks the truth but doesn't harm the adopted child. Even before the child arrives, parents should begin practicing their responses to others, adjusting responses as necessary.

We feel incredibly left out among our friends who have biological children. Our discussions inevitably turn to children. We have nothing positive to contribute to the conversation, since our journey to parenthood has so far been unsuccessful. We have contemplated declining future invitations to get together with our friends because emotionally, it's getting too hard to handle listening to their parenting stories. Do other prospective adoptive parents feel as we do?

Jana Wolff writes in *Secret Thoughts of an Adoptive Mother* that she "made the mistake of joining a mothers' group soon after we got home [with their newly adopted son]," and states that the women in the group discussed breastfeeding woes, "war stories from the delivery" and "weight gains" (108). Wolff goes on to say, "By adopting, I was not a full-fledged mother in their eyes. I hadn't paid the price of pregnancy, hadn't earned the badge of labor or the award for delivery, and would forever be an outsider—an associate member at best. I looked like the other women, but I felt like less of one" (109).

Society makes clear that becoming a mother or father through pregnancy and childbirth is the preferred path. Whether you face intentional or unintentional adoptism (see chapter 4), or if you are feeling less-than because you can't relate to the conversation your friends are having (again), you are getting the same message: You aren't "in" unless you have a child, and you aren't a real parent unless you have a biological child.

First, remember that the friends who are having a parenting conversation are the same people who will be rejoicing with you when you bring your child home. They might be the ones hosting your child's welcome-home party, or the people bringing you meals as you adjust to your first few weeks as Mom or Dad. Second, it's fine to be honest with your friends about your feelings (waiting for "the call" is difficult, for example), but it's not OK to try to put constraints on conversations (like "No talking about childbirth!") because you are waiting to adopt or are considering adoption.

If your feelings are extreme and are harmful to your relationships, counseling might be in order, because you will always be exposed to biological parents discussing their children. You have to find ways to cope with that. Temporary feelings of hurt and jealousy are normal, so you'll have to decide what to do with them. Should you distance yourself from your friends? Do you suck it up and say nothing? Or chime in with humor and honesty? ("I can't wait until I have a little one to wake me up in the middle of the night!") Some prospective adoptive parents volunteer to babysit for their friends' children so that they can enjoy having children around while giving their friends a much-needed break.

It's critical that adoptive parents begin to establish a strong support system prior to adopting. I go into detail on this topic in chapter 8. Adoptive parents face many emotional challenges that are unique to adoption, and having a support system in place helps them cope with challenges in a healthy and productive manner.

I want to adopt transracially, but I live in a predominately White town. Is it fair to bring a brown-skinned child into a non-diverse area?

This is a highly personal decision, and one that shouldn't be taken lightly.

I suggest that you spend a few hours in a neighborhood or town that is predominately populated by people of a race other than your own. Take a walk, dine at a local restaurant, browse a few shops. Observe how people respond to you, and reflect on your own feelings. Consider that any sense of lack of belonging or discomfort will be what your transracially adopted child could face the entire time he or she lives in a predominately White area.

What experienced transracial adoptive parents know is that love isn't enough when it comes to transracial adoptive parenting. No amount of encouragement, hugs, or cheers can negate the fact that the world isn't colorblind. Even neighborhoods or towns that are predominately one race and are accepting of other races cannot change the fact that the faces surrounding the adopted child are a different color, and there will be preconceived expectations, prejudices, stereotypes, and hardships.

If you are dedicated to adopting transracially, you will need to put your child's needs in perspective. Spend some time reading about transracial adoption, and talk to transracial adoptees, fellow adoptive parents, and adoption professionals. Consider whether you are financially able to move to another town and if yes, are you willing to do so for the sake of your child? Remember, your family won't just reside in the town you stay in or move to. Your child will also go to school there, play at parks, engage in extracurricular activities there, shop, and dine.

Another thing to keep in mind is that people tend to be more accepting of babies and young children, but as the child ages, he or she is likely to face increasing prejudice — particularly brown-skinned males. Additionally, as a child enters his or her teenage years, the child will spend more time away from you, which means less time being under the umbrella of your White privilege. The stranger who admired your three-year-old while you were out for a walk with her might someday be suspicious of your thirteen-year-old who walks down the sidewalk with a group of friends.

Questions for Further Discussion

- Review what adoptive parents are not. What beliefs did you hold about adoptive parents prior to starting your adoption journey? Where do you see these misconceptions being perpetuated? Discuss specific ways to address an adoption misconception that comes from a family member, friend, co-worker, or stranger.

- What loss led you to choose adoption? Have you fully grieved it? What steps can you take to begin or continue your healing process? When the loss revisits your family after you adopt, what steps are you prepared to take?

- Review the list of elements for good candidacy for adopting transracially and discuss or reflect on each. What areas in your life need change or further development to better prepare you for transracial adoption?

Practical Application

Gather three colors of beads: black, white, and gray. Black represents brown-skinned people, white represents white skinned people, and gray represents a fairly equal number of each. On a plate, place one bead that best represents the population of the following entities where you live: your neighborhood, your town, your schools, your workplace, your place of worship, your immediate family, your extended family, and your circle of friends. Then spend some time looking at the collection of beads on your plate. Which color dominates? Which areas of your life need examination and racial expansion? In what practical ways can you make changes in your life to prepare for adopting transracially?

Resources for Parents

Adoptive Families magazine

Adoption Nation (Adam Pertman)

Black Baby White Hands: A View From the Crib (Jaiya John)

The Brotherhood of Joseph (Brooks Hansen)

Brown Babies, Pink Parents (Amy Ford)

Choosing to SEE (Mary Beth Chapman)

The Color of Water: A Black Man's Tribute to His White Mother (James McBride)

Inside Transracial Adoption (Gail Steinberg and Beth Hall)

I Will Carry You (Angie Smith)

Secret Thoughts of an Adoptive Mother (Jana Wolff)

CHAPTER TWO

Nesting Without an Egg: Announcing, Waiting for, and Preparing to Adopt Transracially

"It wasn't raining when Noah built the ark."

"It must be recognized that any pre-adoptive training is virtually a drop in the bucket of knowledge. We go to college for two, four, or more years to prepare for a career. We go to pre-adoptive education classes for 20, 24, or 36 hours to prepare for parenting a child who has experienced many insults to his development and beliefs about the world. In essence, we receive less training to carry out the most important job undertaken by adults — parenting!"

~ARLETA JAMES, *BROTHERS AND SISTERS IN ADOPTION*

So you are waiting, but are you ready?

I recall the day we got call from our social worker announcing that we had been chosen to adopt an African American baby girl. My husband looked at me, his eyes wide, and asked, "Are we ready for this?"

Becoming a mother or father for the first time is exciting and frightening. It's natural to wonder whether you are prepared for the task. But when the child coming to you is not biologically yours and does not match you racially, the news that "this is it" is even more overwhelming.

Adoption agencies often do little to nothing to prepare adoptive families for the task of transracial adoption and parenting. Why is this? First, adoption training sessions can be costly and time-consuming for the agency, and many agencies have limited budgets and a small staff. Second, the agency staff may not be well-trained on transracial adoption issues themselves. Third, the authors of *White Parents, Black Children: Experiencing Transracial Adoption* explain that the Multiethnic Placement Act of 1994, "prohibits 'the delay or denial of a child's foster care or adoptive placement *solely* on the basis of race, color, or national origin.' Not wanting to be identified as operating outside the law, adoption agencies continue to have vested interests in not requiring prospective adoptive parents to undergo any type of training for adopting a child culturally and racially different from themselves" (93-94). However, the authors found that of the transracial adoptive parents they interviewed, "They were aware of the fact that to teach about race you need to know about race" (94).

What does this mean for prospective adoptive parents? It boils down to this: If you want to adopt, you need to self-educate, because first, it's your life and your family, and second, for the benefit of your child, you need to be prepared to be a parent in a rare situation.

Despite the torturous time between completing your home study and waiting for a referral or match, the waiting period can be a tremendously beneficial season for the adoptive parent. You make progress, but so much is still unknown. Like a person or couple pregnant with a biological child, the expecting prospective adoptive parent might begin to nest—make frantic preparations for the child or children he or she will come to parent.

Transracial adoptive parents will experience similar nesting routines as adoptive parents adopting a child of the same race; however, preparing for a child of color requires transracial adoptive parents to take extra steps, do more research, and make tougher decisions. Therefore, the waiting period can be a tremendous time of both trial and growth for prospective transracial adoptive parents.

Sharing the Decision

It's natural to be both relieved and nervous to share with those around you that you have chosen to adopt. While you have been preparing yourself to adopt for months, even years—mulling over the idea in your mind, asking questions, reading books, and filling out paperwork— your family members, friends, neighbors, and co-workers have been going about their daily lives. Don't be surprised if your initial announcement doesn't receive a warm welcome. You may be asked questions (including many that would be considered adoptist and racist) and be met with reservations.

I recall reading a post on an online forum once where a woman said, "When my co-worker announced she was pregnant, the office had a baby shower for her and accepted her announcement with glee. But when I shared that I was adopting, there were no gifts, there were no excited bursts of 'congratulations.' I was disappointed, to say the very least."

As discussed in chapter 4, adoption is often viewed in society as second-best or less-than when compared to having biological children. This stems from a lack of adoption education and the societal belief that one's value partially stems from having a biological child and sharing in the biological parent-child-experience with other parents.

Perhaps the most hurtful form of reservation comes from those closest to you—your parents, your siblings, your closest friends. You are excited to be adopting, so why aren't they?

Patricia Irwin Johnston, author of *Adoption is a Family Affair: What Friends and Relatives Must Know*, shares why parents struggle with their child's decision to adopt. She lists reasons such as: "You expected your grandchildren to be born to their parents — your children. You expected them to be genetically related to you and so to be similar in your looks, in personality, in race. You expected them to arrive after a nine-month pregnancy that the whole family would experience vicariously. You expected them to come as newborns. You expected them to 'belong' to your family [...]" (19-20).

Adoption comes with its own concerns, but transracial adoption can be particularly controversial and uncomfortable for some people. It's important that you remain confident and positive — despite any resistance you encounter. Transracial adoption is scary for those who do not understand it, and listening and responding to the concerns of those you love is only the beginning of the trials you will face as a transracial adoptive parent.

With the help of your support group, other transracial adoptive families, your mentor, your social worker, and your personal adoption education, you will learn to deal with reservations from those around you. Chapter 8 elaborates on support systems. This isn't to say you will not feel discouraged or disappointed when you receive less-than-ideal reactions; however, you will be more equipped to deal with resistance and confrontation when you have a support system in place.

You have probably heard that "time heals all wounds." The principle applies to adoption as well. With time (and education), many of those who resisted your decision to adopt transracially will accept and even embrace the idea. Be patient, be firm, and be ever-mindful that the needs of your child must come first.

There are some key individuals who need to know about your adoption plans:

- *Your children.* You want to reveal your decision to adopt to your children in a purposeful, honest, and open manner. This principle is further discussed in chapter 10. It is important that you tell your children you are adopting before revealing the news to almost any other person. Naturally you don't want your children to learn of your plans from someone else. Your children need to hear the news from you, feel that they are "in the loop," and be encouraged to ask questions and share their feelings and thoughts. Get off to a great start by sharing with your children first.

- *Your parents.* Your parents will be the grandparents of your child. Be prepared for that fact that older generations may hold many misconstrued and outdated ideas about adoption, as well as racial prejudices. Be patient, offer educational materials, and discuss adoption openly and honestly.

- *Your siblings.* These are the aunts and uncles who will be spoiling your child with gifts and fun activities. As with your parents, offer education and openness. Answer questions readily.

- *Your friends.* You spend your weekends with them, maybe even vacations. Your friends will be there for you through thick and thin. Don't leave them out of the loop! As with everyone else on your "must know" list, offer education and open discussions on what adoption is.

- *Your boss.* You will need time occasional off from work during the placement of your child. If you are traveling to another country or waiting for a domestic match, you could be asked to travel at a moment's notice. Let your boss know what your situation is, ask what you can do to prepare to leave quickly, if necessary, and find out what the standards are for maternity or paternity leave. Some companies even help with adoption expenses. Promise to keep your boss in the loop should you get any news.

- *Your family doctor.* Depending on the child you bring home, your family doctor might be the primary or referring caregiver of your child. Announcing your plan to adopt also helps establish a more intimate relationship with your physician should you choose to call him or her about a potential child's medical situation. If your doctor cannot help you, perhaps he or she can refer you to a pediatrician or specialist who can.

- *Your local school.* If you are adopting a child who is at or nearing school age, you'll want to research schooling options to seek the best fit for your future child. Questions you might ask could be about diversity, adoption awareness in school projects, special services (should your child have a specific need), and counseling. You need to know up front whether the school you are considering is going to accommodate and encourage your newly adopted child.

- *Your child care provider.* You want to determine if this person or facility is equipped to handle the child you will adopt and whether it is the best fit for your newly adopted child.

Sharing the decision to adopt is a big step for prospective adoptive parents, because it means that the adoption process is moving forward and that someday, possibly soon, your world will change dramatically and forever.

How to Reveal Your Decision

When sharing your decision to adopt with the people mentioned above, I believe it's best to do so in person. This establishes your desire to have an open and personal discussion about adoption. If distance is an issue, consider a video chat.

We were quite nervous about telling our families that we were preparing to adopt. First, we had to be fully committed to the adoption process and be confident in our choice. Once we felt we were, we told our parents and siblings in person. We were straightforward, saying something like: "We have decided that because of the complications pregnancy poses to Rachel's health, we are choosing to adopt."

The best advice I ever received on breaking the news that you have chosen to adopt, especially transracially, is to do so as a statement, not a question. Do not ask anyone's permission to adopt with your announcement. State your decision as a fact. Then, follow up with willingness to discuss concerns and questions. You could give those closest to you books or articles on adoption that might begin their adoption education. Tell them, also, whether you will be sharing the news with extended family and friends, or whether your parents and siblings can do so on your behalf. Keep in mind that when you choose to adopt, your parenting journey begins on that date, not when your child arrives. Begin exercising your own judgment and authority, even during this "expecting" phase.

It's probably best to time your announcement when conversation with extended relatives, acquaintances, coworkers, and neighbors seems to lead to it naturally. For instance, if you're talking to your neighbor about borrowing a chainsaw, you're probably not going to blurt out, "Oh yes, and I'm adopting a child from Uganda next year. I'll have that chainsaw back to you in a week." But if you have a conversation that happens to turn children, announce with confidence that you are about to embark on an adoption journey and would appreciate encouragement and support. As always, be prepared for many questions. Get used to being asked about adoption (often in ways that are not politically-correct).

Some adoptive families have revealed their decisions to adopt in rather creative ways. Some couples send out photos of themselves with a small, empty chair between them with the words "waiting to adopt" printed across the top. I have seen waiting adoptive parents sport t-shirts that say "expecting parents." You could create a video and share it with friends and family.

However you choose to reveal the choice to adopt, do so with confidence, grace, and excitement.

A Plan of Disclosure

When we were first considering adoption, my husband and I sat down with my cousins who had adopted their son from

Guatemala. In our heart-to-heart discussion, they shared with us the joys and hardships of transracial adoption and parenting. "It's important to remember that once you share information about your child, you cannot ever take it back," they warned.

Their insight stuck with me, and as we proceeded through our adoption paperwork, Steve and I developed a plan of disclosure that we re-visited after we adopted our first daughter. What were we willing to share about our child's adoption story, and with whom?

Many seasoned adoptive parents warned me, prior to our first adoption, that certain information belongs to the child, not to the adoptive parents. Therefore, unless necessary, isn't my privilege or right to disclose to anyone.

Such private Information can include:

- Your child's birth name

- Your child's birth parent(s) or previous care giver's age, location, and personal situation (health, finances, etc.)

- Why your child was placed for adoption

- Your child's medical, social, psychological, and emotional history

- Your child's biological family situation, such as if there are biological siblings

When deciding what to share with someone, ask yourself:

- Will sharing this information with this person benefit my child?

- Will sharing this information with this person harm or potentially harm my child?

- Is sharing this information legal? Ethical?

Notice that the center of these questions is the child, as it should be.

It's tempting to become excited about a placement and forget to put the child's needs and privacy first. Especially in the case of transracial adoption, where it is apparent that the family was formed by adoption, adoption itself is at forefront of many questions and comments. If you are adopting a young child, it's also easy to believe that sharing information freely is fine because your child is too young to be harmed by your disclosure.

My research has taught me that I always want our children to learn about their adoptions, first and foremost, from us, their parents. Others who might participate in the adoption discussion are our children's birth parents and siblings, and also our social worker. Eventually, our children might very well ask close relatives or friends' questions about adoption, maybe even a babysitter or teacher, and I want to make sure I carefully choose what I say to these individuals. I want to reveal the complexities of my children's adoption stories to them when I feel it is age-appropriate and in the manner that is most honest and beneficial. You can learn more about discussing adoption with your children in chapter 9.

As you become more comfortable with your child's adoption story and as you learn more about adoption, you will decide what is and isn't appropriate to share with the people in your family's life (and with strangers, too). You owe no one an intimate, novel-length discussion of your child's adoption story.

When a Potential Match or Referral Comes Along

My philosophy is, "Don't count your chickens before they're hatched." Steve and I were both quite secretive about times when our profile was shown to an expectant mother. We understood, from discussions with adoption agencies and attorneys, that a child wasn't ours until all legal matters were complete.

Sharing the news of a potential placement every single time your profile is being viewed or when you inquire about a child can be emotionally draining on the adoptive parent. In the fourteen months we waited for our first child, we had approximately fifteen profile viewings. Each time, we found ourselves nervous and hopeful, and we were disappointed each time we learned we hadn't been chosen.

Every person must decide the best way to deal with potential matches or referrals. As for me, I called my go-to friends including a fellow waiting adoptive mother and a neonatal intensive care unit (NICU) nurse. My fellow adoptive mom friend was someone who understood my concerns, disappointments, and joys, and she didn't constantly bombard me with questions between profile viewings. My nurse friend helped my husband and me to understand adoption situations where the child had (or potentially could have) high medical needs.

Steve and I were so reserved, in fact, that we didn't tell our parents or siblings that we had a placement until we went to court and received official guardianship. We overnighted pictures of our first daughter, a newborn baby, to our parents and waited for them to call us. With our second daughter, right after court we called our parents and grandparents to say, "Guess what?" With our third child, we shard our match-news with just a few family members and friends because our match was two months long and was difficult to keep totally secret.

I'm not suggesting that how we revealed each child's arrival is the best or only way to share. Adoptive parents must decide for themselves when and how to share a match or referral with those around them. If you are adopting with a partner and other children in the home, it's very important that you consider their needs as well as yours. Put up a united front with your partner when it comes to critical decisions. Consider your own emotional health and previous losses. What helped or hindered your healing?

Remember to revisit your disclosure plan, (even just before bringing a child home) and stick to it.

Online Privacy

Technology makes it easy for anyone to share both the most miniscule and the most life-altering occurrences in their lives. In seconds, photos, videos, and posts can be shared (pinned, tagged, etc.) with all your "friends." Adoptive parents must carefully consider what is appropriate, ethical, and legal to share with others, not only in person, but online as well.

As a blogging enthusiast, I often read fellow adoptive parent blogs. One day I received an e-mail from a friend who sent me a link and said, "You are not going to believe this." I clicked on the link and to my shock and dismay, a waiting adoptive couple had posted sonogram pictures of "their" baby (yes, still in the biological mother's uterus), shared details of the mother's situation and location, and even revealed the baby boy's intended name.

I understand that adoptive parents are excited to take on the title of "mom" or "dad." It's a joyful time in their lives. However, unlike parents who answer questions about their biological baby's name and sex and who share sonogram photos, doing either is not appropriate for prospective adoptive parents. It could jeopardize the adoption or future relationship with the biological parents.

I recommend these guidelines to maintain online privacy:

- Do not post photos of someone else without their permission, including on Facebook, Twitter, a blog, a message board, or another virtual community. This is especially true of another person's child–even a child in utero.
- Do not share birth parent, expectant parent, adoptive parent, or adoptee personal information including their location, age, situation, physical description, job title, school, and so on. It is so easy to track down a person with just the tiniest bit of information about him or her. Adoption is a small, small world.

- Remember that once information is shared, it cannot be deleted— electronically or mentally. Even if you delete a blog, a Facebook account, or an e-mail, it is still out there in the virtual world, somewhere, and could be found. Once you share information about an adoption situation, someone will always remember it and can share it, with or without your permission.

- Create pseudonyms when sharing adoption information online. For what information you do share, create fictional names for all the persons involved.

- When participating in an open adoption, have a conversation about privacy with the other parties involved. Decide what you feel is acceptable to share via social media and what isn't. Discuss the fact that the young adoptee, despite his or her age, has a right to privacy of his for her photos and information.

- Check your state laws. As technology advances and the popularity of open adoption increases, the law is gradually catching up. You want to make sure you aren't sharing any information virtually that could lead to a legal issue. Always respect and uphold the terms of your open adoption.

- Use your discretion. Be careful whom you friend on Facebook, whom you follow on Twitter, what you share on online message boards, and whom you e-mail. Is your blog private or public? Treat your online interactions as you would your face-to-face interactions.

Above all, follow the golden rule: Do unto others as you would have them do unto you. Before you type or click or paste, stop and think. Will this benefit those who matter most (my child, my child's biological family, myself) or harm them?

And remember: adoption can be a small, small world. People can easily put two-and-two together to discover names, locations, and details surrounding an adoption situation just from the "here and there" tidbits of information you share online.

Failed Adoption

Failed adoptions tend to be the number-one fear of prospective adoptive parents, and they are not uncommon. There have been international cases where a child passed away before the adoptive parents' arrival or where the parents entered the country to bring their child home, only to learn the child was no longer available. Domestic adoptions sometimes "fail" because the biological parents choose to parent or decide that another family or a relative might be more suitable for the child. It can even happen after the adoptive parents take the child home: a biological parent can revoke his or her parental rights termination documents. When families are fostering children, they understand that the child can be returned to the biological family weeks, months, or even years after he or she was removed from the biological parent's home.

A failed adoption is devastating and can cause an adoptive parent to revisit the grief and loss that led to the choice to adopt in the first place. Some agencies recommend that when an adoptive family experiences a failed adoption, they should take a break from the adoption process to properly grieve the loss of the child. They believe this is in the best interest of the next child who might enter the family.

I highly suggest that you enter any type of match or referral arrangement with your eyes wide open. Understand all the possible scenarios, your legal rights, the child's legal rights, and the biological family's or caregiver's legal rights. Understand who plays what role in the adoption journey — from your social worker, to your attorney, to the child's biological parents or legal guardians, to the court officials. Doing these things will not lessen the blow of losing the child you thought would become yours, but it will help you better prepare your family in the case that a failed adoption occurs.

Remember, a child isn't yours until all legal matters have been properly handled, so be cautious when disclosing information about your match or referral. Carefully consider, as we'll discuss in chapter 10, how you will handle a failed adoption when you have other children in your home.

Questions from the Trenches

I am having a hard time waiting for our child, and it doesn't help that I'm constantly approached by people asking if we've received our referral yet. How should I respond?

People are curious when it comes to expecting families! Similarly, biological parents get questions like, "Are you having a girl or a boy?" "When is your due date?" "Are you having a natural child birth?" "What will you name your baby?" Adoptive parents are even more interesting, especially when the adoption is to be transracial.

One option is to set up a blog (I recommend a private blog) where you share your adoption journey with those you love. E-mail the blog link to everyone whom you want to keep in the loop. If you choose to author a public blog, revisit the online privacy recommendations and your disclosure plan before posting.

Another option is to have a go-to answer that keeps you emotionally sound but doesn't discourage those who care about you from being excited about the adoption. You might say something like, "I hope to receive our referral this summer, but the timing is out of our hands." Or, "I'll be sure to let you know when we get a travel date." You might also thank the person for asking and say, "There's no news to share at this time."

Is it OK to have a baby or child shower prior to the homecoming of our child? I want to be prepared for the child and enjoy the pleasures that biological parents receive when they are expecting.

This is a personal decision. As a type-A personality, I wanted to have a "waiting for baby" shower as soon as we started waiting for a placement. I was eager to register at my favorite baby stores and set up a nursery. Some parents are more reserved and wish to have a baby or child shower after a placement has occurred, which makes sense because then the parent can specify the child's sex, clothing size, likes and dislikes, and even bring the baby or child to the shower to meet family and friends.

Though adopting a child isn't the same as having a biological child, there is no need to set aside your joy. Preparing for a child before or after the child's arrival is part of the parenting process of any parent. If you have someone willing to host a shower for you, go for it!

However, I would suggest not having a shower for a specific child prior to the child's arrival. A general shower is more appropriate. Adoptions fall through, and having bibs with a child's chosen name embroidered across the front will be a painful reminder of what could have been. This is not just the case with domestic adoptions. One adoptive family traveled internationally to adopt a young boy, only to find out the agency had made a mistake and that the boy was promised to another adoptive family! The agency had another child available at a sister orphanage, a girl. They took their daughter home to a blue, transportation-themed bedroom, something they can laugh about now. Adoption is never without its surprises.

On multiple occasions, friends and family members have offered suggestions on how we might get pregnant instead of moving forward with the adoption. We've been asked whether we've tried a special diet or IVF or an herbal supplement to help us conceive a child. Some even say, "You'll adopt and then I bet you'll get pregnant." I'm frustrated that our plans to adopt haven't received the warm welcome I had hoped for.

In chapter 4, I'll discuss adoptism in detail. Adoptism is the belief and expression of the belief that forming a family by adoption is not as good as having a biological child. Adoptism presents itself in a number of ways, including the comments you are facing.

At the heart of these comments is both love and fear. First, those who love you most are going to hurt you the most with their "loving" concern, because their feedback means a great deal to you. You will face comments on your fertility often, so be prepared with a standard response that brings the focus back on adoption. You do not owe anyone an explanation of your fertility issues. A simple, "We are very excited to adopt" demonstrates that you have made your decision and that fertility discussions are off the table.

Second, these comments come from fear. People greatly fear what they do not understand. This, of course, comes down to education and experience. There are many negative and inaccurate stereotypes surrounding adoption in general and transracial adoption in particular. I highly recommend providing family and friends with a list of resources (including this book). Be patient and open. Those who love you most will, most likely, learn to embrace adoption and will adore your child. Remember, Rome wasn't built in a day, and misunderstandings surrounding adoption won't be eradicated in a day, either. Being a transracial adoptive parent requires grace, patience, humor, and stamina.

I'm very excited about becoming a parent for the first time, and I'm going stir crazy waiting. What can I possibly do to help make the wait for my child more bearable?

I am one who loves predictability, structure, and solid plans—everything adoption is not. Waiting was torturous for me, and I quickly realized that I was going to waste many days—even months—if I didn't come up with ways to occupy myself.

First, if you are adopting with a partner, don't neglect that person. It's easy to become child-obsessed, but without a strong relationship, it will be difficult for the pair of you to navigate the ups and downs that come with both adoption and transracial parenting. Invest time and energy into your significant other. Go on dates. Vacation. Take up a new hobby. Go out with friends.

Second, spend some time preparing for your child on your own (and with your partner, if you have one). You can work on cleaning, organizing, and decorating the child's room. Begin to build a library for your child: collect books on adoption, books that feature children of color as main characters, favorite books from your own childhood. When you're out shopping, pick up toys, clothing items, and basic necessities for your child. Enjoy your "waiting for child" shower. Borrow baby name books from your library and explore them. You might also begin childproofing: baby gates, plug covers, cabinet locks, etc. If you are adopting a child with special needs, you can to modify your home with a wheelchair ramp, change the heights of light switches, widen doorways, and so on.

Note that some adoptive parents feel that preparing for a child in advance can jinx the situation. Or for some families, it's simply too emotionally difficult to prepare for a child who isn't yet there especially after losing children through miscarriage, stillbirth, or failed adoptions. If you have such feelings, you can prepare in other ways that don't manifest as physical reminders. Continue establishing relationships with transracial adoptive families, find a support group, widen your circle of friends to include people of your child's race, research hair products.

Third, give to yourself. The saying goes: "You can't give what you don't have." Don't allow yourself to become drained (emotionally, physically, mentally, or spiritually). Remember, your child could arrive at any time—and parenting a child is hard work! Put your best foot forward and take care of yourself. Exercise, eat well, get enough quality sleep, do what you enjoy. More tips on self-care will be provided in the next chapter.

Our first social worker told us, "Don't put your life on hold while you wait for your baby." She was right. The wait is unpredictable, and you could be wasting weeks, months, or even years of your life just staring at your phone or computer screen, waiting for the message that says, "It's time!"

I hate to admit it, but I worry that I won't love my adopted child as much I could have loved a biological child. I'm too embarrassed and ashamed to voice this concern to my social worker and spouse.

I believe it is only natural to question your ability to love an adopted child to the degree you might have loved a biological child (or love a present biological child). Society believes that adoption is "less than," so won't the love be "less than?" Isn't "blood thicker than water"?

Patricia Irwin Johnston explains in her book *Adoption is a Family Affair!: What Relatives and Friends Must Know*, "The truth is that 'claiming' children not genetically related to you may be far easier than you think. [. . .] Perhaps you grew up in a family where the siblings were not much alike, even though it seemed to you that your friends and their siblings had much more in common with one another in looks, likes, and tastes. Perhaps you grew up in a family whose culture dictated that you 'took in' children in need, without ever formally adopting them. If you have not had the opportunity to observe and appreciate diametric differences in personalities and appearance between family members, you may be more challenged in this regard, but you can do it, and you must do so with complete devotion and complete consistency once a little one is adopted into your family" (33).

I don't share Johnston's thoughts with you to discourage you from being honest about your feelings, nor do I wish to simplify adoption, as it cannot be simplified. You can deeply, truly, affectionately, sincerely love someone who is not genetically related to you. Think of your spouse or your best friend.

Granted, falling in love with anyone often takes time. That's why in the next chapter, we'll discuss ways you can work on attaching to your newly adopted child.

My wife and I have faced two failed adoptions and three miscarriages. We desperately want to be parents, but I'm not sure we can handle another major loss. It seems like everyone around us is pregnant or has a new baby. How much more can we take?

You are not alone. Many adoptive parents walked in your shoes. I encourage you to seek support. Isolating yourselves will only deepen your sadness, anger, and confusion. In chapter 8, you can read more about support: joining a support group, seeking counseling, meeting with other adoptive families, and writing down your journey through journaling or a personal blog.

If you feel that you need a break from adoption, by all means, take a step back and regroup. Talk to your social worker or attorney and be honest about your feelings. You need to be fully prepared for the child who does become yours, and entering into the adoption race too quickly will only be harmful to your future child and the well-being of your family unit. It's also OK to take a step back from particularly triggering places and events. For instance, if you (or your partner) can't emotionally handle attending that second cousin's baby shower, decline the invitation.

Continue to be honest with your spouse about where you are at in terms of your feelings and thoughts on adoption. Work as a team to support and encourage each other, and always prompt each other to be open and honest. When you are ready to start waiting again, you want to do so with your best foot forward and in unity.

Questions for Further Discussion

- Make a list of individuals with whom you wish to share your adoption decision. Now, decide whom you wish to speak with first (second, third, and so on) and how to best approach each individual based on your relationship with them. What resources can you share with each person to further their understanding of adoption?

- Review the section on creating a disclosure plan. Make a list of what you are and aren't willing to disclose about your child and with whom. Have you ever been in a situation where you shared too much information and it backfired? How did you feel?

- Review the tips on respecting online privacy. What are some ways you can increase online privacy for you, your family, and any of your child's biological family members whom you have a relationship with?

- How might you prepare yourself, your partner, your current children, and your extended family for an adoption that could potentially fail? What support do you have in place should an adoption not proceed as expected or hoped?

Practical Application

Host a movie night (with or without kids, depending on the film you choose and your goal) where you show a film dealing with the merging of two different cultures. Suggested films include: *Crash, A Time to Kill, My Big Fat Greek Wedding, The Great Debaters, The Help, Our Family Wedding, The Blind Side, Guess Who?, Shrek, The Secret Life of Bees, Jumping the Broom, Remember The Titans,* or *Corrina, Corrina.* Afterward, discuss the film in relation to adopting transracially. Allow those in attendance to honestly express their fears surrounding transracial adoption.

Resources for Parents

Adopted For Life (Russell Moore)

Adoption is a Family Affair!: What Relatives and Friends Must Know (Patricia Irwin Johnston)

Bringing In Finn: An Extraordinary Surrogacy Story (Sara Connell)

In On It: What Adoptive Parents Would Like You To Know About Adoption (Elisabeth O'Toole)

CHAPTER THREE

The Call: Ready, Set, Parent!

"My sheer gratitude that we were moving toward actually having a child was now mixed, on certain days, with a poisonous firing of thoughts that I didn't deserve this gift — that if I couldn't have a baby on my own, the 'normal' way, I didn't deserve to have one at all. People earn a baby by carrying one; the sacrifices of pregnancy make you worthy. My mind offered up this thinking in a kind of serpent-like tongue."

~FROM BRINGING IN FINN, SARA CONNELL

Y ou are overjoyed, overwhelmed, and exhausted. Your child is home, and you are beginning a new adventure. Your world is inside out and upside down, and yet, there are still so many decisions to be made, so much adjusting to be done. Welcome to transracial adoptive parenthood! This chapter focuses on beginning your transition from prospective adoptive parent to transracial adoptive parent.

Attachment and Attachment Parenting

What is attachment, and why is it so important?

Kathleen G. Moss, LCSW, ACSW states, "Attachment is a reciprocal process by which an emotional connection develops between an infant and his/her primary caregiver. It influences the child's physical, neurological, cognitive, and psychological development. It becomes the basis for development of basic trust or mistrust, and shapes how the child will relate to the world, learn, and form relationships throughout life. Healthy attachment occurs when the infant experiences a primary caregiver as consistently providing emotional essentials such as touch, movement, eye contact and smiles, in addition to the basic necessities such as food, shelter, and clothing."

In an adoption, the attachment process is always disrupted to some extent — be it briefly (when the newborn child leaves the biological parents and goes straight into the arms of the adoptive parents), or more extensively (when the child is in foster care or is adopted from an orphanage or an interim caregiver). Moss explains, "If this process is disrupted, the child may not develop the secure base necessary to support future healthy development. Factors which may impair healthy attachment include: multiple caregivers, invasive or painful medical procedures, sudden or traumatic separation from the mother, hospitalization at critical developmental periods, neglect, sexual or physical abuse, prenatal alcohol or drug exposure, and neurological problems."

Why is attachment important? Deborah D. Gray, author of *Attaching in Adoption* explains, "Parent and child attachments are relationships. The quality of parent/child attachments becomes a template for all future relationships and core beliefs" (15). Adoptive parents need to understand attachment, it's importance, and it's future implications, preferably before entering into an adoption, so they have time to learn and prepare.

Shirley Crenshaw, MSW, LCSW, is an attachment therapist with nearly thirty years of experience working with children. She offers these suggestions for adoptive parents and their newly adopted child:

- *Hibernate.* Parents should, if possible, take maternity, paternity, sick, or personal leave from work and use the time off to focus on creating a family unit and helping the child establish a sense of belonging and security. Older children, when possible, should be given an adjustment period before beginning school. Each new situation, even something as seemingly simple as going to church or shopping for groceries, can be a difficult experience for the newly adopted child. Therefore, hibernation time should mostly be spent in the family's home. Crenshaw also suggests that adoptive families put off any non-emergency surgeries for at least six months, because they can cause another trauma in the child's life with dire consequences.

- *Establish.* Parents should establish for their children that they are the primary caregivers and will meet their needs, needs that may not have been met in the child's previous home. For an infant or toddler, this means that the parents should provide the feedings, diaper changes or bathroom breaks, and baths. For children of any age, parents can establish family meal times, family activities, and bedtime routines. Parents need to respond to the child's cries, discipline the child, and provide lots of praise and affirmation. Crenshaw explains that supervision of the newly adopted child is crucial because you can't give a child too much rope and expect them not to hang themselves. Children need structure and boundaries.

- *Touch.* Crenshaw states that positive touch is incredibly important in the attachment process Depending on the child's age and size, consider reading while the child sits on your lap, wearing the child in a sling or carrier, rocking the child in a rocking chair, massage, swimming, co-sleeping, skin-to-skin contact, and adoptive breastfeeding.

- *Expand.* Your transracially adopted child will need to interact with people of his or her race and with other adoptees. Crenshaw explains that the adoptee may have been surrounded by people of his or her race prior to adoption, so suddenly being parented by someone of another race and perhaps being thrown into a new environment where people do not speak, act, or look the same as the people in the child's previous home can be another source of trauma.

Attachment Parenting (AP) has been practiced for many years and among people of several cultures. In the United States, AP seems to be making a comeback. Dr. William Sears and Martha Sears, who are adoptive parents themselves and practice AP, are the authors of *The Attachment Parenting Book: A Commonsense Guide to Understanding and Nurturing Your Baby*. They define AP as meeting your children's needs on a case-by-case (and ever-changing) basis (2). Though adoptive parents yet have little knowledge of a newly adopted child, attachment tools can help foster the learning process. The tools, outlined and explained by the authors, are: birth-bonding, breast-feeding, baby-wearing, bed sharing, belief in baby's cries, balance and boundaries, and beware of baby trainers (5-7). (The term "baby" is used often in the book, as it focuses on infants; however, many of the tools can be applied beyond the infant years.)

I provided merely an overview here. I encourage adoptive families to further explore this topic to gain a better understanding of what attachment is, how to foster healthy attachments, and what to do when a child who needs help attaching comes to your family. There are many books and articles on attachment you can consult.

Adoptive Breastfeeding

One way adoptive parents might choose to bond to their newly adopted infant or toddler is through breastfeeding. Granted, this topic is rather taboo, and you will find that many health care providers, social workers, birth parents, and fellow adoptive mothers are not supportive of this option. Some do not even know it exists. Breastfeeding in general has had a long, controversial history, so you can expect, should you choose to adoptive breastfeed, you can expect to encounter some scrutiny and resistance.

Some breastfeeding manuals touch on adoptive breastfeeding; however, there is, at the time of this book's publication, only one book on the market that is dedicated and fairly current: *Breastfeeding an Adopted Baby and Relactation*, by Elizabeth Hormann. Adoptive breastfeeding is possible and it can be a productive and pleasant way to bond with your newly adopted infant or toddler. But as Hormann explains, "it does require far more patience and commitment than breastfeeding a homegrown baby" (10).

Hormann urges her readers to examine why they wish to breastfeed and whether they have the support to do so. She offers information on herbs, medicines, foods, and hormones that may help the adoptive parent establish a milk supply. Most adoptive mothers are not able to provide their baby with enough breast milk to fully feed the child, so supplementing is often necessary.

The consensus seems to be that adoptive breastfeeding is possible for many, but it can be a time-consuming and stressful process; therefore, having a strong support system, including from your partner and professionals such as your physician or a breastfeeding consultant, is essential.

If the adoptive mother isn't able to establish a milk supply, either because she didn't have the time or knowledge to prepare for the child or her body will not produce milk, a breastfeeding relationship with the child is still possible. As my own adoptive breastfeeding consultant, Dee Kassing, shared with me, breastfeeding is about a relationship, not about milk. Infants have a need to suck, so instead of using a pacifier, some adoptive mothers offer the breast to comfort and bond with the child.

The benefits of breastfeeding are numerous; however, adoptive parents should not let the mission to breastfeed interfere with the ultimate goal: to establish a healthy bond with the newly adopted child.

Choosing a Name

A child might come to you with a birth name, one given to him or her by the orphanage, birth parents, foster parents, or social worker. Adoptive parents question whether it's OK to change the child's name. What if you don't like it, or it's hard to pronounce or spell? What if it makes the child stand out more than he or she already does? What if it's been your dream to give your child a family name? Is a child ever too old to be renamed? Each adoptive parent must decide what is appropriate, necessary, and ethical in the given situation.

Naming your child is an important decision. By naming him or her, you are establishing that you are the child's parent and that the decision to name the child rests with you. Naming your child is also a way to create a sense of belonging. However, many adoptive parents feel that stripping the child of a birth name is undesirable because it might be one of the most important things (or the only thing) the child has that connects him or her to the birth family, birth culture, or previous caregivers. Furthermore, some names have significant meaning. Of course, children quickly become accustomed to hearing their names, so changing a name can be confusing to a child.

Ways to generate a name:

- Work with the child's birth parents or previous caregiver to come up with a name together.

- Incorporate the child's birth name into the name you have chosen. You may wish to make the original birth first name the child's new middle name, for example.

- Give your child a family name.

- Give your child a name that fits with your other children's names, whether the other children are adopted or biological. For example, perhaps all the children's names in your family start with a particular letter.

- Have family, friends, and the other children in your home (if any) help you come up with a name.

- Borrow baby name books from your local library.

- Use Internet sites like nymbler.com.

- View the Social Security's most popular names webpage if you'd like to go with a popular name or avoid anything on the list.

- Use your child's birth culture to inspire a name choice.

Establishing Guardianship in Your Will

All parents should have a current will in place. It's crucial that you decide who will care for your child should you pass away or be in a state in which you cannot carry out your parenting duties. This is no easy decision for many adoptive parents, particularly in the case of transracial adoption. Transracial adoptive parents must consider many factors.

For instance:

- Is the person I'm considering in good health? Does he or she live a healthy lifestyle? How old is this person?

- Is the person financially responsible? (After all, you will likely leave some or all of your assets to this person in order to meet your child's financial needs.)

- Is this person living a life that would be conducive to raising children?

- Does this person have religious beliefs similar to our family's?

- Are this person's morals similar to our family's?

- Does this person live in a racially diverse community/neighborhood that includes people of my child's race?

- Does this person live near enough to our family that the child can remain in the same school, town, or county? If that answer is no, would this person be willing to move for the benefit of my child?

- What type of educational options does this person's community provide?

- Is this person a relative? Will he or she continually and positively help my child interact with other relatives?

- Does this person have an accurate and educated understanding of adoption? Does he or she seem willing to learn more about adoption?

- Is this person willing to uphold any biological-family relationships we've established?

- Is this person married? Single? In a relationship? Does this person have children? Are the children biological, step, or adopted?

In addition, if your child has any unique needs— be they physical, mental, or emotional—you will need to consider whether the person is a good candidate for parenting your child and meeting those needs.

Remember, you can always change your guardianship designation during your lifetime as circumstances change; however, also note that updating your will can be costly.

You might choose to write a letter to the person you are considering establishing as your child's guardian. Agreeing to guardianship is a serious decision. You should be mindful of this, giving the person time to carefully consider your request. In your letter, state your wishes, state what you want for your child should something happen to you, and also, state what sort of financial assets you will be able to offer at this point. It's important that you be transparent about your situation for the sake of your child.

You should also designate a back-up guardian in your will in case something happens to you and the primary person you chose is unable or unwilling to serve as the child's guardian. Asking the primary party occasionally if he or she is still willing to serve as your child's guardian is a good idea. Update your will as your family circumstances change, such as when you adopt additional children, if you divorce, or if your child develops special needs. Likewise, should something change with your chosen person, be willing to find a new guardian, and let the previously chosen person know you are changing your guardianship documents and why.

Post-Adoption Struggles

The arrival of your child is supposed to be one of the most joyous occasions of your life, so why aren't you feeling overjoyed?

In *Adoption is a Family Affair!: What Friends and Relatives Must Know*, Patricia Irwin Johnston explains that besides the everyday parenting stresses of balancing work, play, and parenthood—along with changes in eating and sleeping patterns, and choosing to give up many past freedoms—new transracial adoptive parents deal with worry about relatives and friends accepting the newly formed family. New adoptive parents deal with "insensitive" and "ignorant" questions and comments. Additionally, adoptive parents may not have the same privileges as biological parents when it comes to taking leave from work. Furthermore, being absent from work can "produce anxiety and even guilt" in the adoptive parent (93-94).

Past and present losses also create internal struggles. Johnston shares that "infertility issues resurface," along with sadness that the new child has no genetic relationship to the adoptive parent. She also mentions something that I experienced with both of my girls: parents are overwhelmed at times by the "losses experienced by their child's birthfamily and find it difficult to allow themselves to feel joy rooted in another's grief." She also shares that in a legal-risk adoption, where the "birthparent's decision may be revoked," adoptive parents struggle (94).

In *The Post-Adoption Blues*, Karen J. Foli and John R. Thompson define post-adoption depression as, "A mood disorder that occurs post-placement or post-adoption of a child. Post-adoption depression can be classified as mild, moderate, or severe. The etiology is unknown, but predictive factors include impaired parent-child bonding, lack of social support, and lack of parental preparation. The onset of depression can occur days or years after the child joins the family. [. . .] Post-adoption depression may be episodic, with remissions and reoccurrences" (228).

If you experience any symptoms of post-adoption depression, you should seek professional assistance. You might ask your social worker or adoption attorney for a list of professionals who specialize in working with adoptive families. Fellow adoptive parents might also have suggestions.

Super-Parent

Foli and Thompson say that adoptive parents often have higher expectations of themselves than biological parents because adoptive parents feel they are held to a "higher standard of parenting" because of the "public process" of becoming a family (28). This higher standard can cause a desire for perfectionism and lead adoptive parents to "hide our secrets, our mistakes" (28). And, "withholding feelings often leads to greater isolation and more inner conflict. Emotions become cyclical and self-perpetuating. No one, after all, is perfect. And certainly there are no perfect parents. Our children need to see us as human beings, and when we voice apologies, our children learn that it's ok to make mistakes" (28).

As adoptive parents, we quickly learn that society looks at us in rather polarizing ways. One view, as I mention throughout, is that our family is second-class or less-than, while first-class families are biological ones. Another view of us is that our families are bizarre, exotic, and taboo. Finally, we are seen as "pedestal parents" — saviors, heroes, extraordinary, and special.

When parents adopt transracially, the pedestal grows taller. Images of children in need, be it in advertisements or commercials for hungry or disease-stricken children, almost always feature children of color (particularly, brown-skinned children). The public believes that the neediest children in the world are those with dark skin, and many adoption stereotypes that assume all children who are adopted came from neglectful, abusive, poverty-stricken environments only compound the problem.

Though many adoptive parents insist that they are the lucky ones and are not heroes or saviors, the pedestal-pushing works its way into the subconscious. They realize that they are always being watched, so they sometimes try to act as super parents.

Take, for example, my husband's experience at our local park. On several occasions he took our daughters to the park for an hour after he got home from work to give me some quiet time to write. One evening he returned with the girls and said, "You know, the park is a funny place." I asked him what he meant, and he responded, "I found myself doing what other parents do—praising my kids too loudly, being overly kind, knowing that the other parents were listening." I understood. At the park I had watched parents be one-hundred-percent attentive to their little ones and constantly interfere with their child's play with reminders to "be nice" to the other children, to share, and to "watch out for the little ones." Parents would be patient, gentle, and overly-polite, knowing that other parents were watching. It seemed to catch on like a virus. Parents would loudly praise their child's mildest accomplishments (going down a slide, for example) by cheering, smiling, and nodding. Some snapped photos with their cell phones, begging their children to sit still for a moment and smile for the camera. We would all do it, not wanting to be the parent who lost his or her temper, who grew impatient with our little one's whining, or who came across as anything less than the Parent of the Year.

Transracial adoptive parenting can be just like the park experience, except that the "super-parent" mentality doesn't end when you leave the park. Because our family doesn't match, and because we represent not only adoption but race (both Black and White) and the intersection of these conditions (transracial adoption), we project, we patiently persist, we praise, and we smile.

One area that pressure to super-parent can affect is discipline. Some friends of ours adopted an African American boy when he was a few days old. My friend shared with me that her son entered into a defiant stage when he reached toddlerhood, and she realized she had to crack down on discipline. But she noticed that when she disciplined her son in public by getting down to his level, holding his chin to make him look her in the eyes, and reprimand him verbally, passersby would stare a little too long. She told me it was even more attention-grabbing when her son went through his fit-throwing phases with cries and yells. My friend's solution was to take her son to the car to discipline him, so she could do so authentically and without an audience.

Some adoptive parents feel that they need to be more lenient with their children, because for one thing, someone is always watching and judging. For another, the parent may have waited months or even years for the child, so they want to "go easy" on him or her. Or, in consideration of the child's past (perhaps it was rather dismal or horrifying), the parent decides to discipline lightly or not at all.

As an adoptive parent, you must recognize a few things. First, you are the parent. Despite any skin-color differences between you and your child and the fact that you do not share genes, children need consistent discipline (and praise) to feel secure and to grow up into responsible, mindful adults. Second, you can't let your role as an adoption educator become a priority over your role as your child's mom or dad. Third, though we all code-switch (that is, the way we speak) according to the situation, we don't want to teach our children to act in an inauthentic manner to please or entertain other people.

Letting go of the super-parent mentality and practice can be a struggle for adoptive parents, but doing so allows them to move from being *adoptive* parents to who they truly are: parents.

Self-Care

We've noted that "you can't give what you don't have." The importance of self-care cannot be underestimated.

Transracial adoptive often must cope with unusual and demanding parenting situations. You not only constantly confront adoption-related issues (the public never fails to remind you that your family is different), but you may be parenting a child with special needs (whether physical, emotional, social, or psychological). Maybe you are adopting a sibling group, or perhaps you are accepting a familial placement and tensions in your family are running high.

Whatever the circumstances of your adoption, it's important that you don't put all your "eggs in one basket," your adopted child or children cannot be your only focus. Children are keenly aware of their parents, and children also tend to believe that when things aren't going well at home, it must be their fault.

To be the best parent possible, you need to make self-care a priority. I am a type I diabetic and avid exerciser, and people often say to me, "But I don't have time to exercise or cook a healthy meal." But we all have the same hours in our days, and we choose how to spend them. When I learned that my disease would either help me be healthier—prompting me to eat nutritious meals and exercise —or aggressively and progressively help me become sick, I chose to use the hours in my day wisely so that I could live a long, healthy life. We spend our hours doing what we have decided is most important.

Here are some ways you can care for yourself, so that you can best care for your child:

- *Get enough quality sleep and relaxation time.* Switch nighttime baby feedings with your partner. Hire a babysitter to take your child out of the house for an hour or two each week so you can rest. If your child is too old for a nap, require a daily rest time where the child must play quietly in his or her room while you rest. When I was growing up, my parents designated Sundays for morning church and a family lunch, and then the rest of the day was for resting and relaxing. You might choose to schedule one afternoon a week for leisurely activities.

- *Exercise.* Exercise not only improves your mood, your strength, and your level of energy, it also helps you maintain a healthy weight and gives you a better night's sleep.

Many minority children are at higher risk for diseases like type 2 diabetes (which is highly preventable), so modeling physical activity and including them in it benefits both of you.

- *Eat well.* Despite the general confusion surrounding which diet is the best (Low carb? Raw foods? Mediterranean? Juice fast?), healthy eating really comes down to common sense. Stay hydrated with water, eat plenty of fresh fruits and vegetables, and enjoy whole grains and lean proteins. Again, modeling healthy eating for your children is crucial to their well-being. By preparing and eating healthy foods, you teach your children to do the same.

- *Seek help.* Overwhelmed? Depressed? Confused? Exhausted? Anxious? To combat these, a good start is to sleep better, exercise more, and eat healthier, but sometimes these aren't enough. If you find yourself unable to cope with every day stresses on your own, seek help from experienced professionals.

- *Carve out "me" time.* Many adoptive families find themselves (as many new parents do) totally engrossed in the demands of parenthood and out the window goes any sort of independent, enjoyable adult activities. Schedule a night out with friends, go golfing, grab a book and head to a coffee shop, see a movie with your partner. Do what you need to reconnect yourself and yourself to others (outside of your children).

If you don't possess peace, joy, and patience, how do you expect to earnestly teach those principles to your children?

Marriage Checkup

Deborah D. Gray writes in *Attaching in Adoption*, "Couples often find that they let their own marriage slide for a period of time as they attend to the initial adjustment of a child who arrives with his own set of challenges. The adjustment period can turn into years. Parents can end up with major marital problems resulting from neglected marriage tune-ups. They owe it to themselves to take the time and energy necessary to overhaul their marriage. Even if it means deferring something for the child for a time, putting their marriage at the top of the priority list is healthy" (353).

First, parents should schedule some time alone each day, child-free. As a mother of two very chatty little girls, it's impossible for me to have an adult conversation with my husband when the girls are present. We have found that the best time to talk is immediately after the children go to bed. No television, no cell phones, no chores. We just plop on the couch and talk. After a long day, we reconnect, refocus, and reenergize.

Second, parents need to set time aside to be a couple. Finding a reliable and trustworthy babysitter, be it a family member, friend, or someone you hire, is key. If you know your child is safe and happy, you can enjoy your time off together.

Third, parents who find their marriages facing a particularly rocky time might choose to seek marriage counseling and individual counseling. Because adoptive parenting is a unique challenge, it's ideal that you find a counselor who is educated on adoption.

Adoption alone is complicated and trying for any couple, but throw "transracial" into the mix (and perhaps the adoption of multiples or the adoption of a child with special needs) and couples have every reason to let their marriages fall by the wayside while they meet the immediate needs of their children. However, adoptive parents must remember that if their marriage fails, the whole family will be affected. Additionally, adoptive parents are modeling for their children what a relationship should be.

Questions from the Trenches

My family can't wait to meet our new child, but I'm scared the child will feel distraught and bombarded by all the attention.

When we brought our oldest daughter home, I remember how family members and friends couldn't wait to hold my newborn baby. I remember feeling what I interpreted as leery and selfish. I would cautiously hand my child over to someone, only to feel within a few minutes that I wanted the baby back in my arms.

Part of my hesitation to share my baby is that I was a first-time mom and like most first-time parents, I was overly cautious about germs (it was cold and flu season). However, upon reflection, I realize that my number-one reason for wanting to keep my baby in my arms was that I didn't have a nine-month time period (a pregnancy) to bond with my baby. She was merely plopped into my arms one day, after fourteen months of waiting. I was learning everything about her, from her eating preferences to her sleeping patterns to her physical appearance to her cries. Perhaps it was my motherly intuition that told me I needed to be the primary snuggler of my child. Further, I had read in several parenting books that babies can become fussy if they are passed around from person to person. Naturally, I wanted my child to be content.

Depending on your child's situation, it would be wise of you to put down some ground rules about handling social situations, preferably before the child arrives, but most certainly after. Limit the number of visitors you have and who they are. Hibernate, if necessary. Follow your child's cues. You are adapting, your child is adapting, and you, as the parent, need to initiate opportunities for healthy, safe, and positive adaptation to occur. You don't need to apologize for doing what is best for the child.

Patricia Irwin Johnston suggests ways that loved ones can help the adoptive family (88). They can help with household duties such as preparing meals and cleaning. They can "offer to stay in a hotel" instead of insisting on staying with the family in their home. They can "prepare and freeze some main dishes for the microwave" or pay for a housecleaning service. Johnston notes that new parents often experience the "Cinderella syndrome" where they spend needless time and energy making sure house guests are comfortable which compromises the parents' ability to care for their newly adopted child. Adoptive parents might create a list of suggestions for relatives who want to help rather than turn down offers. Remember, family members and friends often want to be involved. Find ways to help them meet your need and theirs.

Another suggestion is to put together a "welcome home" party, with early invites for relatives and friends. You might schedule the party several weeks or even months after the child's arrival, but setting a date for it gives relatives and friends a heads up that you are looking forward to them meeting your child. By hosting the party and choosing the date, you, as the parent, are in control of who attends, when, and where, fitting it all around your child's needs. Note that a small, comfortable party within the walls of your home might be a better option than having a party in an unfamiliar place.

Remember, you can always use social networking sites or your family's private blog to keep relatives and friends in the loop.

Is it OK to give my child a name that isn't culturally common in his/her racial community?

This is a question I had when Steve and I became open to adopting transracially. In a state of panic, I sent a message to an online friend of mine, a Black woman who was also waiting to adopt. I asked her how culturally important it was that I give my child a "Black" name.

I'll never forget her response. It went something like this: "Girl, name your child whatever you want. A name doesn't make a person more or less Black."

The truth is that I was trying to make sure my child wouldn't stand out more than she already would. I thought that giving my child a particular name would help her assimilate more easily into Black culture. Looking back, I realize that this was rather naïve of me.

When choosing a name for your child, I've noted that there are many things to consider or not. You need to decide what is and isn't important when it comes to naming in your particular adoption situation.

One thing you might consider is how easily a name is to spell and say. As a teacher, I try my best to learn my student's names, but it's challenging when students have hard-to-say and hard-to-spell names. Likewise, a name that appears to belong to a person of a particular race can have its disadvantages, especially with minorities. For example, ask yourself how a particular name might be interpreted on a resume your child presents to a potential employer. Would your child be less likely to receive an interview based on his or her name? (There also might be advantages.) And I'll also say it's easier for me, as a teacher, to remember a student's face when he or she has an uncommon name versus yet another student named Tiffany or Zach.

Once I sent an e-mail to the head of a local Black moms' group. I asked her several questions. At one point, she responded back with, "Are you White? You have a White last name." (The funny thing is, my daughters have the same last name...what advantages of White privilege, will my girls potentially experience due to their "White" last name?)

Remember, it's your child; it's your choice what you name him or her. Take into consideration the factors I discussed earlier in this chapter, and be proud of the name you choose!

Despite my efforts to educate and to initiate adoption conversations, one of my family's close relatives is resistant to accepting my child What am I supposed to do, choose between my child and my relative?

In essence, yes. If your relative refuses to treat your child in a fair and loving manner, you will have to decide between your child and the relative. If you allow the relative to treat the child in a less-than manner, you are making a choice in favor of the relative's poor behavior.

Patricia Irwin Johnston wants relatives of an adopted child to know: "A parent's first obligation will always be to his children. This will be true for your family members who adopt their children. If you are unable to leap with your loved ones into adoption and are therefore unable to treat your grandchildren or nieces and nephews by birth and adoption equally, their parents may be forced by *your* actions or attitudes to withdraw from interactions with you in order to protect their children. This has to happen sometimes. Don't let it happen to you" (33).

Adoptive parents shouldn't use withdrawal from a relative as a threat, but rather as a promise. You should not attempt to scare someone into loving and accepting your child; instead, your focus should be on the child, protecting him or her from interactions that reinforce society's belief that an adoptee (and an adoptive family as a whole) isn't equal in value to a biological family member. Furthermore, you are shielding your child from the reason a relative protests, be it based in adoptism, racism, ageism, sexism, or a combination of these factors. (In fact, we object to prejudice in general. If someone makes a sexist comment, for example, we say something. We want to model for our children that it's not appropriate to discriminate, especially not when it's based on stereotypes.)

At the end of the day, dehumanizing and discriminatory behaviors shouldn't be accepted by adoptive families, no matter who the perpetrator is. Relatives do not receive a free pass to behave inappropriately just because they are relatives.

My child's doctor asked us an adoption question that had nothing to do with my child's medical history. I felt uncomfortable answering, but I did anyway because I felt that the doctor was in a position of power and that I should respect that. What should I do next time this happens?

Professionals, be they doctors or teachers, aren't perfect people, and from my experience, most people, professionals or not, lack adoption education. I recall one doctor's visit where my child's specialist asked, "Do your girls have the same parents?" This question had absolutely nothing to do with the purpose of the medical visit. I remember answering her, because I was caught off guard. I immediately regretted satisfying the doctor's curiosity.

Adoptive parents will inevitably make mistakes along the way. I have learned that when I make one, I should go home, think about the situation, forgive the mishap, and decide how to better handle the situation the next time.

If your child is present is present when you disclose any of the child's personal information, you should apologize for the disclosure and state that you will handle the situation better in the future. This is also a great time to discuss with your child what he or she is comfortable sharing with others regarding adoption at this point in his or her life.

The easiest way to handle inappropriate questions is to ask a simple question in direct response—something like, "Why do you ask?" This puts the focus back on the other person and usually makes him or her realize that the question isn't important to the discussion.

Questions for Discussion

- How can I increase my understanding and practice of bonding with my child?

- Who would make a good potential guardian for my child, according the guidelines in this book?

- In what ways have I tried or have planned to become a "super-parent"? What notions about being an adoptive parent do I need to let go?

- In what ways can I improve self-care?

- Committed couples: What type of relationship are we modeling for our child? What improvements and adjustments can we make within our relationship to better our family as a whole?

- What revisions need to made to the disclosure plan that was put into place prior to the adoption?

Practical Application

Deborah D. Gray, in her book *Attaching in Adoption*, talks about "Fifty Pleasures" (308). She says, "Sometimes life has stopped being pleasurable because all the fun and pleasure items have been dropped [to focus on the child instead of on oneself]," so she recommends that the adoptive parent make a list of fifty things that brings him or her pleasure. These need not be extraordinary or expensive things (like a beach vacation), but rather smaller, everyday things like "going to a movie, putting bubbles in the bath, getting a latte, painting toenails, sleeping in Saturday morning, arranging flowers, making love, poking in a hardware store, looking at photo albums" (308).

Make your Fifty Pleasures list, post it somewhere you will see it every day, and work to make each day pleasurable by doing a few things that bring you joy. Additionally, you might ask your partner to do the same, and then gift each other the time to fulfill one of the things on the other's list.

Resources for Parents

Attachmenttrauma.com

ATTACh.org

Adopting the Hurt Child: Hope for Families With Special Needs Kids (Gregory C. Keck and Regina M. Kupecky)

Attaching in Adoption (Deborah Gray)

Breastfeeding an Adopted Baby and Relactation (Elizabeth Hormann)

Damaged (Cathy Glass)

Our Own: Adopting and Parenting the Older Child (Trish Maskew)

Parenting Adopted Adolescents: Understanding and Appreciating Their Journeys (Gregory C. Keck)

The Ultimate Breastfeeding Book of Answers (Jack Newman, M.D., and Teresa Pitman)

The Attachment Parenting Book: A Commonsense Guide to Understanding and Nurturing Your Baby (Dr. William and Martha Sears)

The Post-Adoption Blues (Karen J. Foli and John R. Thompson)

Theraplay: Helping Parents and Children Build Better Relationships Through Attachment-Based Play (Ann M. Jernberg and Phyllis B. Booth)

Toddler Adoption: The Weaver's Craft (Mary Hopkins-Best)

Resources for Kids

A Family Like Yours (Rebecca Kai Dotlich)

All Families Are Special (Norma Simon)

God Found Us You (Lisa Tawn Bergren)

Happy Adoption Day! (John McCutcheon)

I'm Adopted! (Shelley Rotner and Sheila M. Kelly)

I Wished For You: An Adoption Story (Marianne Richmond)

Max and the Adoption Day Party (Adria F. Klein)

Moses and the Princess (Sophie Piper)

My Adopted Child, There's No One Like You (Dr. Kevin Leman and Kevin Leman II)

My Family (Debbie Bailey)

My New Family: A First Look at Adoption (Pat Thomas)

On The Night You Were Born (Nancy Tillman)

Over the Moon: An Adoption Tale (Karen Katz)

Sweet Moon Baby: An Adoption Tale (Karen Henry Clark)

Tell Me Again About the Night I Was Born (Jamie Lee Curtis)

Ten Little Fingers and Ten Little Toes (Mem Fox)

The Best Family in the World (Susana Lopez)

The Day We Met You (Phoebe Koehler)

The Red Thread: An Adoption Fairy Tale (Grace Lin)

Through Moon and Stars and Night Skies (Ann Turner)

We Belong Together: A Book About Adoption and Families (Todd Parr)

Welcome Home Little Baby (Lisa Harper)

What Kind of Family Do You Have? (Gretchen Super)

Whos Who In My Family? (Loreen Leedy)

CHAPTER FOUR

Are You Really the Parents?: Raising a Black, Adopted Child in a White, Biological World

"Adoption of a white kid would have been enough of a stretch, but we had to go for a baby that not only came out of someone else's body, but out of someone else's culture. What were we thinking? What kind of pseudo-Peace Corps types were we pretending to be? All I could think of was that we were too white to be the parents of someone this black."

~JANA WOLFF, SECRET THOUGHTS OF AN ADOPTIVE MOTHER

I t was a lovely May morning, and my husband and I were pushing our girls in a double stroller across the sand on the Outer Banks shoreline. The air was balmy, the sun was shining, and the waves would occasionally reach our bare feet. Soon we heard a "Yoo-hoo!" and turned to see our beach-house neighbor, a woman in her late-fifties, approaching us to say hello. We had met her the day before when we were collecting shells at low-tide. My oldest daughter, who was quite frightened by the waves, had befriended this woman and had even let her stand beside as the waves rushed over their feet.

The woman joined us on our walk, and at one point we discussed marriage and family. She leaned in and whispered to me, her eyes bearing into mine, "So, you couldn't have your own children?"

This wasn't the first time, nor was it the last, that I have been asked why we didn't have our "own" children. Because we are a transracial family, it's glaringly obvious that we've adopted. The slew of questions from strangers is never-ending and repetitive.

Adoptism

Adoptism, a prejudice experienced by many adoptive families, is when the family (or one of its members) is treated as less-than, second-class, or inauthentic. When combined with transracial adoption, adoptive families might often experience not only adoptism, but also racism; the two frequently go hand-in-hand. Adoptism can also extend into stereotypes of birth parents that further enforces the idea that adoption is second-best and less-than. Birth-parent stereotypes are discussed further in chapter 6.

Much like degrees of racism, there are degrees of adoptism. (However, neither is excusable, no matter how severe the degree is.) Their extent is truly in the eyes of the beholders: those experiencing the adoptism. For me, being asked, "Why couldn't you have your own children?" is one of the more minor forms of adoptism, while being asked, "Why didn't you adopt one of your own kind?" (i.e. a White child) is a more extreme case that reflects both adoptist and racist attitudes.

Transracial adoptive parents will experience adoptism even before an adoption takes place. Family members might ask, "Well, did you try IVF?" or "What about surrogacy?" or "Are you sure adoption is such a good idea? Aren't you scared the birth parents will take the baby back?" Friends might say, "Just wait! As soon as you decide to adopt, you'll get pregnant!"

At the heart of many such comments is a person trying to make sense of adoption, to come to terms with your decision, and to say something well-intended and helpful. However, those in the adoption community will recognize that no matter how "helpful" or loving the commenter tries to be, at the core of the remarks is the person's belief that adoption is second-best to having biological children.

What to Do About Adoptism

When you encounter a comment or question that could be labeled as adoptist, what should you do? There is much you need to consider when responding.

Assess your audience. Who is asking? Is it a family member? A stranger? A friend? Your boss? When you determine your audience, you can better decide how to answer.

For example, a family member who responds to your adoption announcement with, "Have you tried IVF already?" might be processing the loss you are facing by not having a biological child, or he or she might also be facing the reality of his or her own loss of not having a biological grandchild, cousin, niece, or nephew.

Though your initial reaction be to snap at the person, or answer earnestly that yes, you tried IVF (or not), it wasn't even on your radar of options, you might try to relate to the person's potential concerns and offer some education. "Adoption is the best option for our family, and we are very excited to begin the process. I'm sure you have many questions, and we can definitely get together and talk about those." Send the person an adoption article, buy them an adoption book, and keep the conversation ongoing and open. Because you likely have a close relationship with this person, you want to demonstrate that you are willing to discuss the topic further and in more depth.

Now say that a friend of a friend knows you are adopting and says, "I heard you were adopting. My cousin started the adoption process and got pregnant with twins two months later!" Again, the assumption is that having biological children is superior to adopting—an example of adoptism. You can approach the situation with humor and say something like, "Oh, well, we figured we'd have better looking kids if we adopted." Or you can simply address what the person said with, "That's great! Twins!" Or, a general answer: "Great to see you! We are very excited about adopting." You should not feel obligated to share the details of your fertility, your adoption journey, or anything else personal with someone you barely know.

Assess your onlookers. I am approached with adoption questions often, and usually it's when I'm in a public place with my daughters by my side. I am ever-mindful that my girls listen to how I respond to such questions. Likewise, you might be asked about adoption in front of a friend or relative who is listening and learning from you. Whomever you are with, this person is learning how he or she should respond to attitudes about adoption and race from what you say. Therefore, your responsibility is great.

Whether my children are with me or not, I am a firm believer in protecting their privacy, including any intimate adoption-story details. Therefore, I tend to respond with general statements. When asked, "Were their birth parents young?" I say, "Most birth parents, of children adopted domestically are adults, not teenagers." This gives information without divulging into personal information.

You have to decide what you feel is and isn't appropriate to share. I suggest arming yourself with statistics and general adoption information so that when a question arises, you can provide your asker with accurate information that doesn't compromise trust or privacy.

Assess the situation. Many adoptive parents tell me that they can easily tell the intent of an asker. If someone asks a seemingly nosy or adoptism-minded question, some parents respond with, "Why do you ask?" This can render the asker speechless (or stumbling to come up with an answer)—or perhaps it prompts them to share that they are adoptive parents themselves, are considering adoption, or know someone who is.

You then have to decide how (or whether) to continue the conversation. If you are rushing through a store's checkout line, the time isn't right to launch into an adoption education session, no matter the intent of the asker. This would be a good moment to hand the person a card featuring the contact information of your adoption agency, attorney, or support group.

If you have an ongoing relationship with the person who has offended you and your family, it is probably a good thing to confront the person and work to resolve any ill-feelings. For example, we have relatives who had a baby born to them with Down's syndrome. The father said that when things weren't going well for them at work, his co-workers often said, "That's so retarded." The father finally mustered the courage to say one day, "Guys, you know my daughter has Down's syndrome, so I would really appreciate you not using that phrase anymore." The message was well-received and the issue was easily resolved.

However, if adoptism occurs in an outright inappropriate way (such as a teacher discriminating against your child), it's perfectly fine to state that the person is expressing prejudice and, when necessarily, report the situation to a person in an authority position, such as a boss, a fellow parent, a principal, a store manager, or law enforcement.

Prospective, waiting, or new adoptive parents are often caught off-guard by adoptism, but with time, they grow better prepared to face such situations and to confront them with confidence and certainty.

Forms of Adoptism

There are many ways adoptism is expressed, including:

- Labeling a child as "the adopted child" or to announce that so-and-so "is adopted" when it's not necessary to the conversation. Granted, some relatives might be very excited that you have chosen to adopt, but it's still not appropriate, for example, for a grandparent to point out which of the grandchildren were adopted when introducing them. Celebrity adoptive parents are frequently victims of adoptism. Nicole Kidman has four children; her two oldest children, Isabella and Connor, are often qualified as Kidman's "adopted children" in the media. Her youngest child was born via surrogacy, and the media also points out this fact. Pointing out adoptees (and children born via surrogacy) generates reader interest, but it also promotes, if not glorifies, adoptism.

- Asking why the adoptive parents didn't try to conceive a biological child instead of adopting. Such questions might include: "Did you try IVF?" "Did you research surrogacy?" "Did you try an all-organic diet?" "How long did you try to get pregnant?" "Didn't you want your own children?" Adoption is never a decision that parents take lightly, and the circumstances leading up to it are not automatically public information.

- Asking inappropriate and untimely adoption questions in front of adoptees (children) about their personal stories. Questions might include, "Where are her real parents?" (This question assumes that a biological connection is real and implies that adoptive parenting is "fake."). "Does he have any siblings?" "Why did her birth parents give her up?" Some people might question children directly. Children, no matter their age or ability, have a right to privacy.

- Asking about money. "How much did your child cost?" "Isn't adoption really expensive?" "How did you afford to adopt?" One of the more passive-aggressive comments might be: "We've always wanted to adopt, but I've heard it's just so expensive..." Adoptive parents may respond by saying, "If you are interested in adopting, you can call my agency and they can go over all the details with you." You might also tell the asker the adoption process involves the costs of travel, home study, legal fees, and more; the adoptive parent is not buying a child. Sometimes I give askers a range of the total cost for different types of adoption. I never disclose, outside of our adoptive-parent circle of friends, how much our adoptions cost.

- Assuming that all of an adoptee's struggles are a direct result of being adopted. I can recall a few news stories about a teenager who committed a crime where the reporter added, "He was adopted at the age of three." Yes, a child with a troubled past can express negative behaviors. However, not all adoptees are struggling with particular habits or behaviors or situations as a direct or indirect result of being adopted, and not all adoptees were born into troublesome situations. Many children who are with their biological parents struggle in the same ways adoptees do. Parents might often encounter this form of adoptism from medical professionals (such as when the parent asks the doctor about a child's particular behavior), teachers, or even friends and family members.

- Promoting birth parent stereotypes. Not all birth parents are young, irresponsible, on drugs, poor, minorities, or having sex with multiple partners. Again, this is where research comes in handy. Share what you have learned without disclosing personal details.

Most forms of adoptism stem from a lack of adoption education, not malicious intent. However, adoptive parents have a responsibility to confront adoptism directly in the way they feel best serves their family.

Positive Adoption Language

Positive Adoption Language (PAL) is a set of preferred, politically-correct adoption terminology. Examples include using "birth mother" in place of "real" or "natural" mother, saying that a child "was adopted" instead of "is adopted," and stating that a birth mother "made an adoption plan" instead of "gave away" or "put up" her child. Several adoption books and websites offer charts of PAL terms. Using PAL is one way members of the adoption triad can combat stereotypes, avoid hurtful or inaccurate language, and educate others.

Some adoptive families adhere to PAL (in whole or selectively) while others do not. In the March/April 2012 issue of *Adoptive Families*, I published an article called, "Is PAL Too PC?" My argument is that though using PAL is a good place to start with adoption education, sometimes adoptive-triad members use non-politically-correct terms because that is a their own perception of adoption. Although PAL is a unified collection of terms, it doesn't "reflect all of the feelings individual members of the triad have about adoption" (19). I conclude, "We should give ourselves permission to use the terminology that we feel best represents our unique relationships with adoption" (19).

That said, PAL can be helpful when you attempt to combat adoptism. You might offer a PAL chart to family members and friends. *Adoptive Families* online offers free, printable PDFs. PAL alone will not resolve adoptist attitudes, but it is a good tool to combine with resources and experiences.

Adoptism + Racism = A Whole Lot of –ism

Adoptism is a frustrating prejudice to encounter in and of itself, but when others compound adoptism with racism, it can be even more frustrating for transracial adoptive parents. Adoptism and racism together create a double-edged sword.

On spring afternoon, I was with my girls and we saw an older African American lady holding an infant. My youngest daughter was in an infatuation-with-babies stage, so we meandered over to say hello. While my girls doted on the baby boy, the grandmother and I talked about the beautiful weather and the ages of the kids. She asked, "Are they A-D-O-P-T-E-D?" (I suppose she was trying to be sensitive by spelling it out.) I said yes, and her reply was "God bless you" (three times over).

I wasn't sure what she meant by her "blessing." Was she affirming my choice to adopt? Was she astounded that I would dare parent two African American children? Did she assume they had been adopted from an abusive, neglectful household or that I had brought them home from a decrepit orphanage? What had she faced in her life that would prompt her to "bless" my decision? Did she mean to warn me or compliment me?

The fact is, transracial adoption is complicated. Yes, it starts with the desire to have a family and the adopted parent and child relationship grows with love and trust. However, there's a big bad world out there that seems, as times, to be determined to belittle and dehumanize transracial adoptive families.

Adoptive parents need to arm themselves with plenty of support (see chapter 8) and resources to give them the energy and education to continually combat adoptism and racism. Likewise, you and your child should have an open and ongoing dialogue about adoption and race as he or she gets older.

It's Ok to Say "Black"

People who have little experience with those of other races might be shy to approach the subject of race. In my experience, I have heard Whites in conversations about race say, in a whisper, that a person being discussed is "Black." Race has become a taboo topic in society because everyone is afraid of offending someone else. However, when you adopt transracially, you do not have the luxury of ignoring racial issues. It's glaringly obvious that your child doesn't share your skin color.

Elisabeth O'Toole, in her book *In On It: What Adoptive Parents Would Like You To Know About Adoption*, writes, "Within our families, we know our loved ones as so much more than their race. But that doesn't mean that racial differences can simply be dismissed. It is an important aspect of our loved ones, among many important aspects. [...] It's important that the child's own experiences and racial identity, separate from that of his family, be valued and affirmed" (81). She also notes, "One of the great privileges of adoption, particularly transracial adoption, is that it offers all of its participants opportunities to broaden their understanding of other people's life experiences and to connect with people and communities they might not otherwise. [...] this is another unanticipated gift that a child may bring to the family" (81-82).

Understandably, many White people don't talk about race, nor are they comfortable doing so. Beverly Daniel Tatum writes in *"Why Are All the Black Kids Sitting Together in the Cafeteria?": And Other Conversations About Race,* that she when she asks her students to "reflect on their own social class and ethnic background," minority students are quick to answer while White students aren't sure how to respond. One student in particular said, "'I'm just normal!'" (93). Tatum concludes, "Like many White people, this young woman had never really considered her own racial and ethnic group membership. For her, Whiteness was simply the unexamined norm. Because they represent the societal norm, Whites can easily reach adulthood without thinking much about their racial group" (93). She continues to say, "There is a lot of silence about race in White communities, and as a consequence Whites tend to think of racial identity as something that other people have, not something that is salient for them. But when, for whatever reason, the silence is broken, a process of racial identity development for Whites begins to unfold" (94). For new transracial adoptive families, bringing a non-White child into the family might be the first time other family members have been challenged to think and talk about race.

Adoptive parents should set the precedent that it is OK to discuss race and racial issues. They should embrace incorporating the child's race into the family's life. This is further explored in chapter 11. Adoptive parents who were once part of a White-only family find themselves newly defined as a Black-White family. Approaching this new identity can be challenging, but with education, openness, and humor, families will find themselves growing more comfortable and confident.

Questions from the Trenches

I expect to face some adoptism and racism from Whites, but I wasn't prepared to encounter adoptism and racism from Blacks.

I guess I thought that because my child is "one of them," they would readily accept my family.

When we first brought home our oldest daughter, I was terribly nervous around African Americans. I desperately wanted them to dote on my daughter and affirm my husband's and my decision to adopt a Black child. What I found was that we experienced racism and adoptism from people of many races, ages, and geographical regions.

In some racial cultures, adoption is less acceptable than in others. The adoption agencies I've spoken with rarely see the placement of Hispanic children, for example. In some racial cultures, such as those of Hispanics and Blacks, familial and unofficial adoptions are far more common than in other racial cultures. If a member of the culture cannot take care of a child, a relative, such as a grandparent, aunt or uncle, or cousin might step in as caregiver. There can be a lot of shame in placing a baby for adoption, formally and with strangers.

When someone of your child's race makes a comment that implies adoptism and/or racism, the comment might stem from the cultural belief that a person who places a child for adoption, particularly outside the family and with people of another race, acts outside cultural norms and should be frowned upon.

I remember stopping at a well-known tourist restaurant on our way to Tennessee for a vacation. My daughter and I sat on one side of a booth, my husband on the other. The waitress, a Black woman, said to us, "I cannot imagine giving my child away. I have a two-year-old son. I could never give him to someone else." You can decide for yourself what that implied: adoptism, racism, or simply a woman trying to fathom how a mother could "give" her child to adoptive parents.

Also, remember that Whites have a lengthy and rather gory history of treating people of color in dehumanizing and degrading ways. Blacks have good reason to be untrusting and skeptical of Whites, especially when it comes to Whites raising "their" children. I do believe that society's views on transracial adoptive parenting is changing, but that's because transracial adoption is becoming increasingly common and, most definitely, transracial adoptive families are becoming more willing to discuss transracial adoption and promote adoption education. I write often on the subject of transracial adoption both in articles and on my blog, and many comments that I receive from members of the Black community are supportive and positive.

At the end of the day, adoptive parents need to be confident in their decision to adopt and to instill family and racial pride in their children. There will never be a perfect world where adoption and race aren't called into question.

One of my family members consistently uses negative adoption terminology that is hurtful to me and my child. I'm afraid that if I confront the person, I will offend her. However, I can't imagine this terminology continuing to be used in front of my child!

When a family member struggles (knowingly or unknowingly) with adoption and/or race, it's best to deal with the situation, no matter how uncomfortable, for the sake of your child. No matter who is uttering improper language or spewing harmful stereotypes, you must, as the child's parent, make the person aware that his or her actions are hurtful and inappropriate. I believe it's especially important to make those closest to your family aware of inappropriate language, because it's likely such a person will spend a significant amount of time with your child.

It can be incredibly awkward to confront a relative, especially if the offense has been taking place for quite some time. However, better late than never!

Decide how you wish to approach the person: in person, via e-mail or a letter, or with a phone call. Do what is most comfortable for you. However, keep in mind that tone is hard to determine in an e-mail or letter, so sometimes a phone call or in-person conversation is best.

Be direct, be polite, and most of all, be open to forgiving. You might say something like, "When our family gets together, we have a wonderful time. However, I've noticed that you often refer to my son as the 'adopted' one in the bunch. Though I'm sure you are proud of the fact that he is part of our family, labeling him as 'adopted' ostracizes him. The place I want my son to

feel the safest and most accepted is when he's among family."
I can tell you as a writing teacher that starting with a positive
comment (family gatherings are fun) before moving into more
serious topics helps ease the listener into your concerns. Being
direct is important (state the exact offense and why it is hurtful)
to avoid any confusion. Then, end with another positive ("I'm
sure you are proud of the fact that he is part of our family.").

Give the person a chance to respond. It's possible he or she
had no idea that the terminology being used was offensive. The
person may, on the other hand, become defensive. If this occurs,
listen to the person and respond; however, don't waver or apologize for standing up for your child. Remind the person that you
both have something in common: you love and care deeply for
the child.

If necessary, offer resources to educate the person on adoption: articles, books, blog posts, podcasts. Don't be afraid to admit
your own past failures, either. Perhaps you frequently used
improper adoption terminology or made assumptions based on
a person's race. Share that educating yourself helped you become
a better parent and member of the adoption community.

*I got really upset the other day when I read an article on
transracial adoption where the author ended by asking, "Can
Whites effectively raise Black children?" Sometimes I feel that
my ability to parent my child is always been called into question
because we're not the same race.*

I guess my answer to the question is: yes, it's possible. Any
parent *can* effectively raise any child, despite the child's race, but
parenting transracially involves much more than just everyday
parenting.

Transracial adoptive parents should recognize that parenting brown-skinned children involves not only parenting them
and raising the children to become successful, independent,
responsible, and kind adults, but also instilling in the children
racial pride and an understanding and acceptance of the child's
racially cultural norms, racial reality, and history. These might
include hair care and styling (see more about this in chapter 5), an

understanding of White privilege and discrimination, and a focus on Black history. Though a child might be in a White family, he or she is Black, will always be Black, and will often be held to racial standards, especially when he or she is older and isn't always with his or her parents. Therefore, adoptive parents need to prepare their child for life as a person of color, not as a White child.

You have probably heard the saying, "Don't get mad; get even." If you aren't Black, you'll never be Black. You can't change the fact that you weren't born racially matching your child. Therefore, you have to work extra-hard to understand and promote Black culture in your home for the benefit of your child. There will always be critics. What matters most is what you do with your energy. You can pour it into justifying your family, or you can channel your energy into doing what is best for your child and meeting his or her needs.

My children are old enough to speak for themselves. Should I let them respond to adoptist and racist comments, or should I take the reins?

When someone utters a racist or adoptist comment or question, we have to remember that our role, above all, is to provide for, protect, and support our children. One morning I took my girls to the local park. A fellow mother asked if my girls were "real sisters." Before I had a chance to respond, my creative and funny three-year-old piped up, "We are not sisters! We are brothers!"

Every child and situation is different, which is why it's important that parents keep an ongoing and honest conversation with their children about discrimination. Ask your child what he or she would like to see happen in an uncomfortable situation where there is prejudice. Would he or she like to speak up? Should you step in? How should the situation be handled? It would be wise to run through different scenarios with your child to prepare the child in advance. Scenarios can be from real-life, or you might use a news story to prompt discussions.

It's also important to discuss situations after they occur and see if any revisions need to be made to your response plan. Perhaps your child is going through a shy stage or has recently been questioning adoption. Modify the plan as often as necessary. You might even have a code word or gesture with which your child can give you permission to answer a question or combat a racist statement.

I don't think parents should ever justify a hurtful asker's actions; however, you might use a particular situation, such as an eighty-year-old White man using the word "colored" when referring to Blacks, to speak to your child about history and change. Negative situations open up doors of communication for parents, allowing us to teach and guide our children.

One of my adoption mentors and fellow adoptive mother gave me some great advice once: use opportunities to discuss adoption or racism with your children, even when the situation doesn't involve your child, such as a news story or an incident on the playground. Show your child that the conversation is always open. Don't wait for your child to insist on discussing adoption or racism with you (which may never happen); be proactive and open with your children.

Questions for Further Discussion:

- What adoptist comments or questions do I frequently encounter? What are some standard responses I can give next time? When have I responded poorly in the past?

- How much of my journey to choosing adoption am I willing to share with my family? Friends? Co-workers? Neighbors? Strangers?

- What does my personality suggest about how I might respond to adoptist or racist comments? Am I sarcastic? Shy? Aggressive? Private? Outspoken?

- When I respond to an adoptist or racist comment, what is the best way to respond that will resolve the situation while protecting my child?

- Is there anyone in my family, in my circle of friends, at my workplace, or elsewhere who has hurt me with comments or questions about adoption? What is the best way to confront the person to achieve the desired result?

- What unresolved issues am I experiencing that are hindering my confidence as an adoptive parent? What or whom can help me resolve these issues productively?

- How am I preparing my child to face adoptism and racism?

Practical Application

Discuss politically correct terms for people of different races and politically correct adoption terminology. Based on your experiences and your geographical location, how do terms heard in your area differ from the politically correct terms? Generate a list of terms your family is comfortable using and discuss why you choose to use this terminology.

Resources for Parents:

I'm Chocolate, You're Vanilla: Raising Healthy Black and Biracial Children in a Race-Conscious World: A Guide for Parents and Teachers (Marguerite Wright)

In Their Own Voices: Transracial Adoptees Tell Their Stories (Rita J. Simon and Rhonda M. Roorda)

Love in Black and White: A Memoir of Race, Religion, and Romance (William S. Cohen and Janet Langhart Cohen)

White Parents, Black Children: Experiencing Transracial Adoption (Darron Smith, Cardell K. Jacobson, Brenda G. Juárez)

Resources for Kids:

A Mama for Owen (Marion Dane Bauer)

A Mother for Choco (Keiko Kasza)

All Families Are Special (Norma Simon)

Families Are Different (Nina Pellegrini)

Horace (Holly Keller)

It's Okay to Be Different (Todd Parr)

Little Pink Pup (Johanna Kerby)

Quackenstein Hatches a Family (Sudipta Bardhan-Quallen)

The Cow That Laid an Egg (Andy Cutbill)

The Gingerbread Girl Goes Animal Crackers (Lisa Campbell Ernst)

The Little Green Goose (Adele Sansone)

The Thunderstruck Stork (David J. Olson)

True Story:

In March of 2012, Dana Newman and her family of eleven children experienced delayed entry into the Little Rock Zoo in Arkansas. An employee claimed that Newman's family, consisting of two biological and nine adopted children of various races, couldn't use the family pass unless they could prove, by showing adoption decrees, that they were a real family. After thirty minutes, a supervisor allowed the family to enter the zoo and later told a local news station that the zoo had seen daycare businesses attempt to use family passes to admit their group of unrelated children. Therefore, employees had been told to watch out for businesses trying to take advantage of family passes.

CHAPTER FIVE

Crown of Glory: Hair (and Skin) Care

Gaze around playgrounds, supermarkets, and restaurants and you will see Black children with a variety of hair styles ranging from dreadlocks, to afros, to braids accessorized with beads, to puffs, to buzz cuts, to cornrows. Some styles are intimidating—they appear to be extraordinarily complicated and time consuming. How is a transracial adoptive parent, one who has perhaps never even touched Black hair before, supposed to ensure that his or her child's hair is properly maintained?

Many of the prospective parents I have consulted with seriously contemplate not adopting transracially due to their intimidation surrounding the care of Black hair. These parents understand that Black hair culture is complex, historical, and crucial to the racial identity and acceptance of the Black, transracially adopted child.

With any aspect of transracial adoption, knowledge is power. When prospective and adoptive parents invest in educating themselves on Black hair, the payoff is rewarding.

This chapter will provide you with an overview of Black hair and skin, but it's not intended by any means to be your be-all, end-all guide. As with anything related to transracial adoption, you will start somewhere and then continue your research over the course of the adoptee's childhood.

Hair

Washing and Conditioning

When my oldest was young, I made the mistake of washing her hair far too often (like every other day) and using traditional baby products, such as all-in-one washes, to care for her hair and skin. Over-washing, over-combing, over-styling, and generally, over-touching black hair can lead to hair breakage and dryness. The jury is still out on exactly how often Black hair should be washed; however, it definitely seems to vary from child to child and hair type to hair type.

It's important to note that White hair care products are not made for Black hair. For one thing, Whites often seek to remove moisture from their hair, while Blacks wish to maintain as much moisture as possible. Therefore, White hair care products are typically quite drying and strip the hair of product build up and natural oils. And, just because a product is labeled for Black hair, doesn't mean it's the best one for your child's hair type. Descriptions of hair types, along with illustrations, can be found on Rory Hadley's blog *Chocolate Hair, Vanilla Care*.

Like anything else, hair products range from inexpensive to very pricy. Do not gauge what you should buy or spend based on what you might spend or use on your own hair. Nor should you be lured into purchasing expensive products because you believe you will "get what you pay for." Further, be open to trying other products as your child's hair needs will inevitably change.

Cutting and Trimming

Black hair must be trimmed to maintain its health and hold its chosen style. How often this needs to be done varies from child to child. Adoptive parents will be able to determine a hair-trim or cutting schedule as they get to know their child's hair. If a child comes to you with hair that has been extensively damaged or neglected, cutting it, instead of giving it a mere trim, might be the best course of action. Another option is hair dusting: trimming the hair so slightly that "dust" appears on the floor instead of balls or chunks of hair.

It is important to find a salon or barber shop that is experienced in working with children of your child's age and is familiar with Black hair. Ask for salon and barber shop recommendations from members of the Black community. You may opt to cut or trim your child's hair yourself if you feel confident enough to do so.

Some in the Black community support the idea that a Black child's hair, particularly a Black boy's hair, shouldn't be cut until after the first birthday. This is a cultural norm, and adoptive parents may choose to follow it or ignore it.

Styling

Adoptive parents have several options for styling their Black child's hair. Styles range from fairly simple, such as puffs or twists (both favorites in my household) to more intricate styles such as braids and dreadlocks.

If you wish to style the child's hair yourself, you'll want to attend hair shows, observe styling techniques online or in person, and practice frequently. Hadley's website offers parents directions for creating a practice styling board. Learning to style Black hair can be frustrating and time-consuming. Do not be discouraged when the style doesn't turn out exactly as you had hoped. Practice makes perfect!

Or, you may opt to pay someone to style your child's hair. Research local salons and barber shops, and don't be afraid to state directly that you want someone who is well-experienced in working with Black hair and children of your child's age. If you see someone in public whose child has a cut or style you or your child admire, approach them and ask who cut or styled the child's hair.

Another option is to hire someone to come into your home and style your child's hair. Your child may not be ready to go visit a bustling beauty salon or barber shop. (Some children, due to past medical or abusive trauma, may find a salons or barber shop environment particularly frightening or over-stimulating). The benefit is that your child is probably comfortable at home and will be in familiar surroundings while his or her hair is being styled. This might be particularly helpful when your child has just come home or has faced a rather traumatic past.

As you experiment with various styles, you will find those that work best for your child's hair type, age, preference, and activity level.

Training Young Kids to Sit During Styling

Young children and children who are extra active have a hard time sitting still. Transracial adoptive parents, too, have quite the challenge teaching their young ones to sit still for hair styling sessions. The following techniques are suggestions on how to encourage your children to be patient at styling sessions.

Try these suggestions to ease the process:

- *Have a routine place to style hair.* We style our girls' hair while they sit on stepstools in front of a favorite movie. The routine helps the child get comfortable with the styling process. Other parents put young kids in highchairs with a snack. Some prefer to style hair surround by mirrors while the child sits on a vanity stool or chair.

- *Choose your styling time wisely.* Do not style hair when you are rushed or when your child is hungry, tired, or sick. Likewise, choose your style according to the time you have available. Some parents like to schedule a weekly block of time for hair-styling.

- *Let your child choose the style.* I'll ask my daughter how many puffs or braids she would like, or I'll let her choose between two styles (braids or puffs?). Give your child a hand mirror so he or she can observe the styling process.

- *Create a positive experience.* Hair styling can be an uncomfortable experience as you work through your own learning process and as the child is asked to turn in different directions (sometimes awkward ones) as you work through his or her hair. Talking to your child, being patient, and being willing to take breaks when needed will help your child see hairstyling time as a normal and pleasant routine. Read your child books about hair from my resource list.

Let Kids Be Kids: Deliberate Exercise and Physical Activity

Recently, I have read about the prevalence of Black women choosing not to exercise due to the negative impact it has on their hair. Not working up a sweat may keep their hair intact, but the health risks outweigh the benefits. Minorities, including Blacks, have a much higher risk of particular diseases, such as type 2 diabetes, and exercise is an avenue to help prevent some of these devastating illnesses.

That said, it's critical that you allow your child to be active so that he or she not only maintains a healthy weight at this stage, but also to establish healthy behaviors that continue through their adult years. As much as it might bother you to watch your child's three-day-new-hairstyle become disheveled after a gymnastics session, don't discourage the child from participating in physical activities. There are many ways to protect Black hair including swim caps, silk scarfs or bandanas, and protective styling.

Diet

Black children not only need to eat healthy so they can learn, play, and sleep well, but also to grow and maintain healthy hair (and skin). Children should always be well-hydrated with healthy drinks, including plenty of water, and fresh fruits and vegetables, which have a high water content. A diet which includes plenty of healthy fats (like the Mediterranean diet: fish, olive oil, etc.) has been said to help with hair and skin.

Because children of color are more likely to develop serious conditions such as heart disease and type 2 diabetes and many of these conditions are related to a person's dietary choices, parents are wise to condition their children early on that a healthy diet is essential to not only looking good but feeling good as well. Of course, the best way to encourage children to eat a healthy diet is for the parents to set a good example. As a family, grocery shop, prepare meals, and eat; these activities encourage and motivate children to make healthy dietary choices.

Special Hair Situations

Head Lice. Can Black children get head lice? The answer is yes, they can, but it is rare. (However, there are many different types of Black hair, some more readily house lice than others). Many schools do head-lice checks, and many rule that all children must be checked despite the unlikelihood that a Black child will have lice. Ask your child's teacher to notify you in advance of any head lice screening dates, so you can determine what to do in advance. Perhaps you'll attend the screening with your child to make sure his or her hair is inspected in a way that doesn't damage hair. You also want to be prepared so that you can send your child to school with a hairstyle that accommodates the screening.

Picture Day. Some schools give children cheap combs on picture day for touching up hair before the session. You will know in advance when picture day is (since the photography company wants you to buy a photo package), so you can prepare accordingly by talking to your child's teacher about your child's hair. Be clear that you do not want your child using the comb (depending on your child's age or circumstance) or anyone else using one on your child.

Overnight Visits/Slumber Parties. Whether your child is going to visit grandparents or having a slumber party with friends, you'll want to prepare the adult in charge. Lay down the ground rules with your child (don't let anyone style your hair, wear your sleep cap, etc.) and with the adult. Send whatever hair supplies necessary to Grandma's house (along with instructions) if any hair maintenance is necessary. Don't forget the child's swim cap or sleep cap if used. Little girls can be encouraged to participate in other activities besides hair styling (such as painting their fingernails), so that all the children present can be included.

Cradle Cap. Black babies can get cradle cap, which is more difficult to deal with when the child has kinky, curly, or wavy hair, where flakes can easily stick. An easy and natural way to remove cradle cap is to rub olive oil on the affected areas and gently brush, comb, or wash out flakes. Do not try to aggressively remove cradle cap; you do not want to damage your child's scalp. Also, do not over-wash or over-comb the child's hair.

Sand. We learned the hard way that sand and Black hair do not mix well—or, should I say, they mix so well that you can't get the sand out! We put a sun hat on our daughter at the beach when she was almost two. We had reminded her not to remove her hat, but she managed to whip it off and dump a bucket of sand onto her afro. She had sand in her hair for over two weeks after that. If you choose to take your child on a beach vacation, consider using a swim cap to avoid any sand incidents. Sandbox play can also be challenging, so parents will have to determine if the risk of a sand-in-hair incident is worth the opportunity for children to play in sandboxes.

Buckling-In. Babies, toddlers, and preschoolers spend much of their young lives strapped into car seats and strollers. Many of them are covered in fabrics intended to be durable and long-lasting which is hard on Black hair. Inexpensive satin pillowcases can solve the problem. Simply place the pillowcase over the head-area of the child's car seat or stroller for protection. Satin sheets can be purchased for your child's crib or bed.

Skin

Just as there are many different Black hair types, there are many different shades and conditions of Black skin. Some children cope with a slew of skin issues such as eczema, while other children have baby-soft and evenly-toned skin. As a transracial adoptive parent, you will be offered a lot of advice regarding your child's skin, but remember, "one size" never fits all.

Bathing

A common mistake among transracial adoptive parents is bathing their Black child too often and for too long. Black skin tends to be dry, and sitting in a bathtub of water often and for too-long spurts of time will only increase the problem.

How many times to bathe the child during any given week depends on your child's skin and activity level. In the summer, fall, and spring, my girls bathe approximately three times a week, as we tend to be outside a lot and they get dirty. In the winter, we bathe our girls twice a week. Parents may opt for sponge baths (a simple wipe-down with a washcloth) between regular baths.

Long, too-warm baths without immediately moisturizing afterward can increase skin dryness. Baths are an enjoyable experience for many children, but it's wise to establish early on that baths should be kept reasonably short, and the water should be warm but not hot. Older children should be encouraged to keep their shower water at a reasonable temperature.

To soften your Black child's skin naturally, add baking soda and food-processed oats to your child's bathwater. (It is not recommended that you add these ingredients to jetted bathtubs).

Moisturizing

A person's skin is his or her body's largest organ. Skin is porous; therefore, the body is essentially ingesting whatever is put on the skin.

There are many lotions available; some of these are strongly marketed to the Black community who often suffer from dry skin issues. However, recent research, along with the going-green movement, has revealed that because the beauty industry is highly unregulated, ingredients in many mainstream beauty products are considered mildly to moderately dangerous, especially when used over many years.

Some of the most dangerous and ambiguous ingredients in beauty and personal care products include parabens, sulfates, and fragrances. "Fragrance" is a catch-all term that discloses nothing about the actual ingredients that are used to make the product smell attractive to the consumer. Parabens (which act as a preservative) have been linked to certain cancers, including breast cancer. Sulfates (foaming agents) can cause dryness (the exact opposite effect you are aiming for when moisturizing or cleaning your child) and skin irritation.

Thankfully more and more beauty companies are going-green (and organic) with all (or at least some) of their products. Doing your research and learning to read ingredient lists will help you choose the best lotion for your child. It's important to note that "natural" is not a regulated term, so beauty-product companies use it freely and hope you will not understand that "natural" really doesn't mean anything.

If you wish to avoid the risks of commercial beauty products, turn to your kitchen. Coconut oil and olive oil are two safe moisturizers. Some kitchen oils combine common allergen oils (almond oil or sunflower seed oil) with the primary oil. Read the ingredient list carefully to avoid placing potential allergens on your child's skin. Moisturize the skin immediately after a bath and as frequently as you see fit.

Eczema

The Mayo Clinic reports that eczema, also called atopic dermatitis, has been said to be one of the top three skin conditions to affect African Americans. Eczema is usually characterized by dry, irritated patches of skin, most commonly in fold areas such as the inner elbow and behind the knee, though patches of eczema can be anywhere on the body. When scratched, the patches can become irritated and even infected, creating more discomfort.

The exact cause of eczema is unknown, though it may be due to some genetic factors as well as allergies, asthma, and the environment. Visits to a dermatologist and allergist would likely be helpful. Treatment might involve topical or oral medications, special therapies, creams or lotions, bleach baths, or wet compresses. Other options include avoiding traditional detergents, taking short and mild baths or showers, and properly moisturizing skin.

Treating eczema, like any other medical condition, often involves trial and error. Adoptive parents could benefit from communication with the child's birth family, if possible, to see if there is a genetic connection or knowledge of a common allergen that can aid the parents in making decisions involving treatment. In the case of my oldest daughter, we discovered that two of her biological relatives also suffered from eczema. Eliminating cow's milk from her diet, as one family member did, nearly eradicated the condition. Lactose intolerance is arguably more prevalent in Blacks and Hispanics than in Whites, though the exact links between eczema, allergies, immune system weaknesses, asthma, genetics, and other conditions is confusing and intricate.

Diaper Rash

Black children can get diaper rash. Due to their darker skin, it can be more easily missed than a rash on a White child. Remedies include changing the baby's diaper more often (and immediately after a dirty diaper), changing diaper brands (there may be a sensitivity or allergy to the diaper's chemical content) or switching to cloth diapers, and applying a store-bought or homemade diaper cream. If the rash persists, seek medical attention for your child to rule out other conditions and to pursue a more aggressive treatment.

Scratches, Bites, Acne, and Scars

Darker skin shows scratches, bug bites, acne and scars quite prominently. My youngest daughter scratched her forehead with her finger one day and though the injury was minor, the line across her forehead remained for nearly two months, showing obviously against her dark brown skin. My older daughter's eczema patches are dark in color and can remain visible on her skin for weeks after the eczema itself has cleared.

There are many over-the-counter and prescription treatments for various skin issues; however, as mentioned before, many of their ingredients can be undisclosed and unhealthy, particularly for Black skin. (Some creams can cause the skin to appear bleached or lightened.) Adoptive parents can research alternative and natural treatments (applying honey or vitamin E, for instance) and weigh the benefits of these treatments against traditional solutions.

Sunscreen, Sunburns, Tans, and Vitamin D

Yes, brown-skinned people can get tans, sunburns, and even skin cancer. However, brown-skinned individuals have more melanin in their skin, which acts as a natural sunscreen, so they do not face as many sun-related dangers as do lighter-skinned people.

Should you put sunscreen on your child? The answer is: yes and no. Traditional sunscreens can contain the same potentially harmful ingredients as other beauty products. Alternative sunscreens are available as well as recipes to prepare your own sunscreen.

With the increase in sunscreen usage (no doubt a result of the skin cancer rates) and people spending less time outdoors, Americans are suffering, as a whole, from a vitamin D deficiency. Vitamin D is produced in the body as a result of the skin being exposed to sunlight. The Mayo Clinic reports that the deficiency is a probably especially dark-skinned individuals, because the darker the skin, the less vitamin D the person produces. Vitamin D is responsible for bone health, as well as aiding in the prevention of some major diseases such as type 2 diabetes, some cancers, and heart disease (all of which are more prevalent among African Americans). A simple blood test can determine a person's vitamin D level.

In our family, we follow some general guidelines to help our children get some sun exposure (important for vitamin D) while not over-exposing them to the harmful rays that can lead to sunburn and, in the future, skin cancer. We do not swim or play outdoors during peak sun hours (middle of the day). When we are playing outdoors or swimming during off-peak hours, we do not wear sunscreen. Once a year we go on a beach vacation; due to the sun's intensity, we wear a "healthy" sunscreen, limit our sun exposure, and wear protective clothing such as sun hats.

Do your research on skin safety and consult medical professionals as you make choices for your brown-skinned children.

Questions from the Trenches

What is the best response to a person (be it a stranger, family member, or friend) who attempts to touch my child's hair?

Black hair is mysterious to many, particularly people who are White, and typically, Black hair is inaccessible to them. When a transracial, adoptive family appears, some see this as an opportunity to satisfy their curiosity. Oftentimes without warning, a stranger, friend, or family member will reach out and touch the Black child's head and follow with a comment or question. (Never, I will note, has a Black person touched my children's hair, as it seems to be an unspoken rule in the Black community that hair-touching is off limits). It is possible that the offender is being adoptist by touching your child. As the authors of *Real Parents, Real Children* note, many people "view adopted children in general as somehow not 'belonging' to their parents in the same way genetically related children do," which "creates an atmosphere in which any adult can feel freer to exert authority over an adopted child or disregard personal boundaries — especially by touching the child — well beyond the toddler years" (178-179).

Some adoptive parents want to say "Hands off!" to the offender, yet they do not want to appear rude or unfriendly. It can be an uncomfortable situation for the parents and especially for the child (who does not wish to be touched).

First, remember that a child — no matter his or her age — is a person who deserves privacy, personal space, and respect. To be touched, as if he or she were a pet, can be offensive and is inappropriate, especially when the touch comes from a stranger or someone the child is not familiar with.

Second, a stranger should not touch a child. Children should be taught from an early age that he or she never has to accept uninvited touch from anyone, including strangers, and that in fact, such touch can be dangerous to the child's safety and well-being. Adoptive parents who might be excited about the attention his or her child is receiving from the public might bypass common sense and encourage the child to allow his or her hair to be touched; however, this can set a dangerous precedent for the way the child perceives strangers.

Third, Black hair is fragile and time-consuming to care for and style. Friction, dirt, and oil from the hands of hair-feelers can break, damage, dirty, or fray styled hair.

An easy response to someone who attempts to touch your child's hair is to intercept the touch, either by moving the child or moving yourself slightly in front of the child. This should be hint enough that you do not wish the person to touch your child's hair. Another response is to prepare your child to respond by saying, "Don't touch my hair." It is perfectly fine for the child to be direct and vocal about his or her body and personal space. Since my oldest daughter was two, we have practiced with her to say, "Don't touch my hair. I don't like it."

When it comes to those you know well, be it the child's grandparent or a favorite neighbor, generating a response that is direct but not offensive can be challenging. I have found that e-mailing articles to the offender on the difficulty of caring and styling black hair tends to not only send the message that your child's hair should not be touched, it also educates those close to your family on Black hair. Another option is to share with them a story of when someone touched your child's hair and why it was offensive and bothersome.

Overall, remember that your child didn't choose to be the race he or she is, nor did he or she choose to be adopted transracially and to be thrust into society's spotlight. He or she should not be forced to entertain the curiosity of others. And despite the fact that many adoptive families openly educate others on adoption, a line must be drawn to protect the safety and personal space of the adopted child.

How should I respond to unsolicited hair advice from a person of my child's race?

Steve and I were once at Target. My daughter, then only six months old, was sitting in the cart babbling and chewing on a toy while we pushed her around the aisles in search of a greeting card. We were approached by two Black women, one of whom said, "That baby's hair is dry."

My inner mama-bear came out, and I was immediately offended by their comment. But I didn't have time to respond because the women began offering me suggestions on moisturizing hair products and then lotions for my baby's skin. Before I knew it, Steve and I were following the women through the store as they pointed out various products to us.

Looking back, I realize that the women were not seeking to offend us. They were offering advice that was meant to better my child's physical appearance and her acceptance in Black society.

As you will learn, there are numerous products for black hair and skin, as well as many different hair and skin types and conditions. There is no one magic product; and you will likely go through much trial and error to find something that works for your child. You won't always get it right, but you have to start somewhere.

You can respond to unsolicited advice in a number of ways ranging from sarcasm to docile nodding to anger. However, I have personally found that though I know my child best and I am her mother, I may not always know the best way to care for her in certain areas, hair being one of them. Just as I seek a doctor's advice on caring for my daughter's asthma, I need to be willing to accept experience, suggestions, and wisdom from others when it comes to my child's hair.

Not all advice you receive will be helpful. However, learning to listen and be grateful for suggestions will only benefit you and your child in the long run. By being respectful of others and their experiences, you are teaching your child to do the same—hair related or not.

By engaging with strangers, I have made connections that have benefitted my children. I have found someone to braid my daughters' hair, I learned about a blog that offers tips on styling and washing, and I gained helpful suggestions on natural hair products for my children's different hair types.

What if someone refers to my child's hair as "good," "bad," or "nappy"?

One Sunday at church, a woman approached my family, looked at my daughters, pointed to my youngest and said, "She's got the good hair." ("Good hair" in the Black community is generally defined as hair that easy to manage; it typically refers to hair that is straight, loosely wavy or curly, or soft). Part of me was offended, as if this woman were saying that one of my daughters was beautiful and the other was ugly, but part of me also understood that the woman meant to compliment my youngest daughter and voice that straighter, softer hair is more manageable.

The term "nappy" is offensive to some Blacks; however, some use the word to empower and embrace Black hair culture. I always find that when in doubt, using more politically correct terms is best. Words to describe Black hair such as kinky, curly, or wavy are more readily accepted, particularly when they are used by a White person. (I often hear the argument that if Black people can use a certain word, such as "nappy" or "nigger," then White people should be able to use it too. However, Whites have a long history of treating Blacks as subservient, if not in an outright degrading and dehumanizing fashion, so it seems appropriate that Whites, whether they have personally acted in a racist manner or not, avoid terminology that might offend some members of the Black race.) The easiest response to the word "nappy" is to state the word you use in your home—be it kinky, curly, wavy, or something else.

When deciding how to respond to someone who makes a statement about your child's hair, consider the geographical cultural norms and dialect of where you live as well as how you wish to represent transracial adoptive families and, most immediately, your own family. Is your goal to educate? To dismiss nosy comments? To correct? To reinforce? To ignore?

I recall thanking the woman who commented on my youngest child's hair. We didn't want to continue the conversation, nor did we wish to make a big deal of it, so as not to reinforce the idea that my oldest daughter's hair is considered more difficult and less "good" than the baby's. Sometimes a simple "thank you" for a compliment is the easiest way to wrap up a conversation and move on. However, if your child is older, you might wish to discuss an incident once you get home. How did your child feel about being complimented? What about the other children who didn't get the same compliment? Depending on your child's age, reading one of my suggested resources to him or her would be helpful.

As with any questions transracial adoptive families face, it is best to discuss situations, like hair comments, at home and decide how your family will respond the next time a question is asked. If a child is old enough, he or she might choose to respond. Younger children will need their parents to handle the situation tactfully and carefully. It is perfectly understandable that adoptive families grow frustrated and annoyed at the constant slew of strangers who feel the need to share their opinions, but when you are prepared in advance to face such situations, you will leave conversations feeling satisfied and proud that you remained calm and composed.

A stranger approached me and asked if my child is full or mixed. How should I have responded?

It's important that we teach our transracially adopted children to be proud of who they are and of their racial backgrounds. Eventually, your child will decide what race(s) he or she most identifies with and which race box or boxes he or she will check on official paperwork. The color of the child's skin in relation to the race(s) the child claims will no doubt be a persistent issue throughout his or her life, as well as the fact that his or her skin doesn't match that of his or her parents. Bi-racial or multi-racial children potentially face even more identity issues and colorism as strangers try to put them in a particular "box." For example, President Barack Obama has faced criticism for stating he is Black when many believe he should state that he is bi-racial.

A person asking if a child is "full" or "mixed" is more than likely trying to figure out your family's situation (how you came to be a family). You can respond by either stating the child's race using politically correct terms (he is African American, she is biracial, etc.), ignore the asker altogether, or respond in another manner your family has decided upon.

If your child is old enough, he or she may wish to respond to the asker. A black woman I know who is an adoptee said she despised the question: "What are you?" People often wanted to know her racial makeup and how she fit in with her adoptive family. She generated a response that put the askers in their place: "I am human!"

Someone made a comment about how dark my child is, and then said it two more times! I don't know what to make of this comment or how to respond.

Sometimes people express observations about your child's skin to prompt you to tell them whether the child was adopted, where the child was adopted from, or the race of the child's biological parents. Again, you have to decide as a family what the appropriate response will be in such cases. If your child is old enough to answer for him or herself, he or she should decide how the situation should be handled. This is always easier to discuss in advance at home.

Colorism, much like racism, is still alive and well today. We hear sayings like "The blacker the berry, the sweeter the juice," but they are belied by public sentiment. Darker-skinned models are repeatedly passed over in favor of lighter-skinned Blacks on magazine covers, on television shows and movies, in advertisements, even in the skin tones of children's toys such as dolls and action figures. Even when medium or darker-skinned model is used, his or her skin is often technologically altered to be lighter. The "look how dark your baby is" comment could be a sign of colorism.

Sometimes the easiest response is just to say, "Thank you" (even if the person hadn't intended to compliment you or your child) and move on. You dismiss without allowing further inquiries.

A child at my daughter's school said my daughter's skin was "ashy," which really embarrassed my daughter. How should we respond?

Blacks tend to have dry skin that is difficult to keep moisturized, even when parents are diligent about skin care. Like my oldest daughter, some Black children suffer from eczema, which increases dryness and creates irritated patches that cannot be quickly fixed by a smear of lotion.

Send a well-proven lotion to school with your child so she can moisturize her own skin throughout the day, such as after exposure to outdoor elements during recess or PE class. I also suggest that you investigate further to see if your child is being bullied. Prompt your child to share with you any past issues with other students (or any that might occur in the future) and talk to your child's teacher about them.

In public, I've had a stranger remark how "cute" (handsome/ pretty/adorable) my child is—multiple times. The situation gets awkward. How should I respond?

Sometimes people do not know how to react to a transracial family, so they go to what seems safe: a compliment. But overstating that your child is cute (or handsome, pretty, or adorable) is uncomfortable. You wonder, "Is this person fishing for adoption information? Is he or she questioning if the child is mine? Is this person racist and is attempting to cover it up?" We don't usually know the intent of the person questioning, complimenting, or insulting our family. Nor do we need to. As the child's parent, you feel a need to dissipate the awkwardness, and you can do so in a number of ways.

I think the best way to handle a "cute" comment made one too many times is to thank the person and walk away from the conversation. (Once, my family was in a checkout line at a store. A woman turned and asked if my girls were sisters. I said, "Yes." She persisted by asking again, rephrasing her question: "Were they sisters when you got them?" I looked her and said, "They are *real* sisters," and then I took my children out of the store while my husband finished paying for our items. I did this to avoid further conversation with this woman and to protect my children from her ignorance). If you are in a place where you cannot get away from the person— say in a check-out line at a store— change the subject. You can point out an item in his or her cart that you've used and liked, you can talk about the weather (how cliché, I know!), or you can simply turn your back to the person and start loading your items onto the counter. You could even take a fake cell phone call. Get creative. Just remember, you don't owe an explanation or your family's entire life story to anyone.

It's important that as your child's parent, you compliment the child for talents, abilities, and strengths, not just good looks. (Our new bedtime routine with our children is to compliment them individually. I tell my oldest, for example: "You are smart. You are creative. You are beautiful. You are funny. You are silly.") You, unlike the stranger approaching your child, are aware of your child's positive attributes; therefore, you have the responsibility and the honor of praising the child for these things.

My teenage child is determined to try a new hair style, one I'm not a fan of. What should I do?

You want to help your child fit in with his or her peers within reason. If your fifteen-year-old was asks for a tattoo, well, that's a permanent mark on the child's body that he or she may not appreciate several years down the road. But the beauty of hair is that it can be changed.

Teenagers need to exercise some control over their lives as they near adulthood; this is how they learn responsibility and learn about positive and negative consequences to the choices they make. You may not like the hairstyle your child wants, but allowing him or her to decide on it builds the ability to take pride in his or her appearance, fit in with peers, and make decisions.

Minority hair care can be costly. If you cannot afford to or choose not to pay for the services your child desires, you might negotiate finances. You could offer to fund so much hair care per year with the child funding the rest, or you might decide that the child must fund the entire service himself or herself.

Dealing with a teenager, so my friends tell me, is all about negotiation, patience, and grace. Hair is just a small factor in many challenges parents of teens face. Choose your battles wisely, focusing your persistence and power on more major issues such as where to go to college, sex education, etc.

Questions for Further Discussion:

- What are some practical steps I can take to better my knowledge of Black hair?

- If I'm approached by someone who makes a comment about my child's hair, be it positive or negative, how will I respond?

- If someone uses a word, such as nappy, to describe my child's hair, how will we respond?

- How do I feel about being offered unsolicited advice about my child's hair? How might I respond to it?

- If a stranger attempts to touch my child's hair, what will I do? What if it's a family member or friend?

- What are some steps I can take to better understand how to care for my child's skin?

- Should I have my family's vitamin D levels tested?

- If someone makes a comment or asks a question about my child's racial makeup, how do I intend to respond?

- Have I approached my child to see if he or she is experiencing any bullying issues at school, especially in regards to his or her hair or skin? How have I prepared my child if he or she encounters a bully?

Practical Application:

Watch Chris Rock's *Good Hair*, a documentary on Black hair, with your partner and older children. Discuss what "good hair" is in today's society. Ask your children: What hair struggles have you faced? How do you feel about your hair? Use this time as an opportunity to compliment your children on their many wonderful attributes: their talents, their personalities, their gifts.

Watch Disney's *Tangled* as a family. Talk about the role Rapunzel's hair played in the film. How was it both a blessing and a curse? In what ways do your younger kids enjoy their hair? What about their hair bothers them? Another option is to read the story of Samson in the Bible and discuss it.

Resources for Parents:

Good Hair (DVD)

Hair Story: Untangling the Roots of Black Hair in America (Ayana Byrd and Lori Tharps)

It's All Good Hair: The Guide to Styling and Grooming Black Children's Hair (Michele N-K Collision)

Skin (DVD)

Textured Tresses: The Ultimate Guide to Maintaining and Styling Natural Hair (Diane Da Costa and Blair Underwood)

Blog: www.chocolatehairvanillacare.com

Resources for Kids:

All Kinds of Children (Norma Simon)

All the Colors of the Earth (Sheila Hamanaka)

The Barber's Cutting Edge (Gwendolyn Battle-Lavert)

Bintou's Braids (Sylviane A. Diout)

Bippity Bop Barber Shop (Natasha Anastasia Tarpley)

Chocolate Me! (Taye Diggs)

Cornrows (Camille Yarbrough)

Corn Silk and Black Braids (Vincent L. Johnson, M.D.)

Ella Kazoo Will Not Brush Her Hair (Lee Fox and Jennifer Plecas)

Fancy Nancy: Hair Dos and Hair Don'ts (Jane O'Connor)

Haircut at Sleepy Sam's (Michael R. Strickland)

Hair Dance! (Dinah Johnson)

Happy to be Nappy (bell hooks)

I Like Me! (Nancy Carlson)

I Love My Cotton Candy Hair (Nicole Updegraff)

I Love My Hair (Natasha Anastasia Tarpley)

I Won't Comb My Hair! (Annette Langen)

Mirror, Mirror, Who do YOU see? (Norma J. McCandless)

Nappy Hair (Carolivia Herron)

Nina Bonita (Ana Maria Machado)

Saturday at the New You (Barbara E. Barber)

Shades of People (Shelley Rotner and Sheila M. Kelly)

Something Beautiful (Sharon Dennis Wyeth)

The Hair Book (Graham Tether)

The Skin You Live In (Michael Tyler and David Lee Csicsko)

Utterly Lovely One (Mary Murphy)

Whose Knees Are These? (Jabari Asim)

Whose Toes Are Those? (Jabari Asim)

Wild, Wild Hair (Nikki Grimes)

"I Love My Hair" Sesame Street Video Clip from YouTube

True Story

During the 2012 Summer Olympics, many news outlets focused on the criticism gold-medalist and Black teenager Gabby Douglas faced from the public, via social media sites such as Facebook and Twitter, for having her hair pulled back in a ponytail and secured with clips during her many gymnastic performances and news appearances instead of wearing a "good" hairstyle.

CHAPTER SIX

Two Mommies, Two Daddies: Navigating Open Adoption

"Birth parents and adoptive parents both care about the same child. They are not in competition for the affections and loyalty of the child. Parents can care about more than one child, and children can care about more than one set of parents"

~BETSY KEEFER AND JAYNE E. SCHOOLER, TELLING THE TRUTH TO YOUR ADOPTED OR FOSTER CHILD

Many adoptive parents, even some families adopting internationally or from foster care, face the decision of whether to have an open adoption. What is open adoption? What are common fears? Is open adoption harmful or helpful for the adoptee, the birth parents, birth relatives, and the adoptive parents? What might an open adoption look like? Open adoption can be an overwhelming choice and journey; however, with education, you can make a healthy and informed choice.

Defining Open Adoption and Its Prospective Benefits

There are three categories of adoptions: closed, semi-open, and open. The definitions of these terms are arguable, but for the sake of discussion, I will define them generally. A closed adoption, or a confidential adoption, is one with no ongoing communication between the adoptive family and the birth family. The adoptive family has limited information about the birth family and probably the child as well.

Semi-open adoptions are those where the birth and adoptive family communicate within limits, such as in letters and pictures exchanged through an intermediary like the adoption agency or adoption attorney. The adoptive family has at least moderate information on the birth family and the child due to this more open relationship.

Finally, open adoptions are those where the adoptive family and birth parents correspond directly (through snail mail, texting, phone calls, social media, etc.) and may even visit one another. Some open adoptions include spending holidays together (possibly including the child's birthday), additional extensive and frequent visits throughout the year, and sharing in birth or adoptive family celebrations (such as the adoptive family attending the child's birth mother's college graduation ceremony). Open adoptions might also include extended birth family members: grandparents, aunts and uncles, siblings, cousins, etc. There is usually more contact between parties in an open adoption than in a semi-open adoption.

Open adoption, when positive and possible, gives adoptive families, birth families, and the adoptee access to information that can benefit everyone. Such information might include:

- Medical history and current medical issues

- Family history (names, traditions, stories, etc.)

- Personal information (hobbies, likes and dislikes, struggles, changes, and so on.)

There can also be:

- Racial role modeling

- Friendships and other supportive relationships

- Extended relationships, between birth and adoptive relatives (siblings, grandparents, cousins, aunts and uncles)

Fearing Open Adoption

Steve and I have spoken about open adoption at several adoption training sessions. Many families elect a semi-open adoption only, due to their many fears. When adoptive families consider open adoption, relatives, friends, and even strangers often resist because of birth parent stereotypes, news stories they've heard, and personal insecurities. All this to say that open adoption isn't a decision adoptive families take lightly. In fact, they face much resistance.

Open adoption is resisted because of the fear that:

- A biological parent may try to "take" the child back

- Having two sets of parents may confuse the child

- The child may want to return to the birth parents and reject the adoptive family

- Other children in the family may be jealous of the extra attention open adoption bestows upon one child

- Jealousy could arise between parties

- Open adoption is unpredictable (i.e., fear of the unknown)

- The adopted child may feel hurt if the birth parents choose to parent prior or subsequent children

- The adoptive parent has less control over the child (i.e., competes with the birth parents for the child's affection and loyalty)

All of these concerns are valid, and adoptive parents should be honest about their motivation to have, or not have, an open adoption with the child's biological family. It's important to keep in mind that not only will some adoptive parents struggle with open adoption, but the "Other" in the situation, often one or both of the child's biological parents, might struggle as well.

The Other

Society often dehumanizes and demonizes birth parents, mostly because they are misunderstood. Adoptive parents are often not immune to feeling this way about birth parents. First, the media powerfully conveys that birth parents are not to be trusted or respected because they are immoral people. Second, adoptive parents are glorified; they are the "winners" in the situation, and if there's a winner, many people believe there has to be a loser. Thirdly, many adoption agencies and attorneys do little to educate adoptive parents about birth parents because the focus of these entities tends to be on what the adoptive parents want, because they are the ones paying for the service. Additionally, adoption agencies and attorneys may believe birth parent stereotypes or neglect to educate themselves on birth parents; therefore, these adoption professionals are unable or unwilling to pursue educating adoptive parents.

Learning about birth parents can be incredibly life-altering for adoptive parents. While preparing to adopt, a birth parent is the person providing the family with the child. But when adoptive parents come into contact with an actual birth or expectant parent, they are able to "put a face to a name." At the minimum, when an adoptive family is matched or referred, they realize they are committing to a child who wouldn't exist without the birth parents.

Just as adoptive parents must face some sort of loss in order to adopt, and just as adoptees face loss in their lives, birth parents also experience tremendous loss. This includes the fact that even in the most positive and open adoptions, birth parents forever live with the loss of their biological child. Elisabeth O'Toole notes, "Anniversaries and holidays—the child's birthday, Mother's Day—are often very difficult" (43). These dates, which are supposed to be celebrated with food, gifts, and gatherings, serve as powerful reminders of the birth parent's loss. I once spoke with a birth mother who shared that she often feels as devastated as a mother whose child goes missing; the mother knows the child is "out there," but the loss remains unresolved, causing heartache, distress, and confusion throughout the mother's life.

The fact is that adoptive parents must recognize that their gain (a child) only comes from the birth parent's loss, a loss that a birth parent never "gets over" or "moves past" (despite what agencies often promote and adoptive parents like to believe). Granted, each adoption situation is unique, and each birth parent reacts to the loss of a child differently.

Birth parents are often the most forgotten and minimized members of the adoption triad; however, they are, at least initially, the most powerful in the adoption journey. I suggest that adoptive parents explore resources that enhance their understanding of the birth parent perspective, starting with Ann Fessler's *The Girls Who Went Away* and including *The Open Adoption Experience* by Lois Melina and Sharon Roszia. Such resources can help adoptive parents navigate adoption in general, open adoption, and discussions with their adopted child.

Establishing an Open Adoption

Open adoption is legally enforceable in a few states. In most, the adoption professional (agency or attorney) and the birth parents expect the adoptive family to honor the promises they make to the biological family members. It's important to note how incredibly frightening it is for many birth parents to have to rely on the adoptive family to hold to the open adoption agreement.

First, adoptive parents should educate themselves on open adoption before entering into any adoption. Understanding what open adoption is (and isn't) empowers the adoptive parents to make an informed decision about whether open adoption is a good decision for their family or not. It's important to be honest with your social worker or attorney about your feelings and questions regarding open adoption.

Once the family has decided that an open adoption is a good choice, the next step is to assess the adoption situation that comes their way. Based on the information provided to the adoptive parents, is it healthy and safe for the child, and for the entire adoptive family, to enter into an open relationship? Remember, all relationships take time to develop, so open adoption doesn't have to be an all-or-nothing and sudden experience.

Next, with the assistance of your adoption professional, establish what open adoption might look like for your family. (It's important to involve all family members in this exploration). Likewise, the birth family should express what they hope for out of the adoption. "Open" might mean something very different to you than to the birth family. If your child is old enough, he or she will also want a say in what type of relationship he or she desires.

Options in an open adoption might include:

- An exchange of e-mail addresses (some adoptive families set up an e-mail account or private blog just for communication with the birth family)

- An exchange of phone numbers and/or addresses

- Becoming "friends" on social media websites

- An exchange of photographs

- An exchange of information

- Visits (How often? Where? When?)

- Gatherings (Birthday celebrations, holidays, etc.)

You may also wish to discuss who can attend visits. Is it OK to bring family members, friends, or significant others? Do you want an adoption professional present?

Remember to consider online privacy (see chapter 2). Is being "friends" on a social media site a healthy decision for the child? What limits should be established? If you choose to be online "friends," consider that the child's photos and other information will be displayed to many people, including many you will not know, who can view them and share with others.

Finally, come to an agreement on the openness of the adoption. The agreement doesn't have to be permanent. You might agree to a certain time frame for which your agreement is valid and then re-visit it later to make revisions.

Updates

Many adoptive parents in open and semi-open adoptions send updates to the birth family, sharing information about the child. Updates may be sent via e-mail, snail-mail, or through a private blog. These updates can be incredibly stressful and daunting for adoptive parents, especially those who wish to appear to be super-parents (see chapter 3) and those who are sensitive to a birth parent's struggle to place the child for adoption.

Updates may include:

- The child's growth (height, weight) and clothing size (to demonstrate growth)

- What the child eats and how much

- Details about language development (new words, favorite or funny sayings, etc.)

- Fact about physical development (New tooth? Learned to kick a ball?)

- Unique experiences (A trip to the zoo, family vacation, etc.)

- Firsts (First word, first smile, first trip to the pumpkin patch, etc.)

- Favorites (Foods, activities, friends, etc.)

- Dislikes (Diaper changes, eating veggies, etc.)

- Hardships (Illness, stage of defiance, unique challenges like biting, etc.)

Some adoptive parents are leary to share hardships about their child with the birth parents for fear that they will appear to be failing parents. After all, the child was probably placed to be given a better life than that which the birth parents could provide at the time. However, it's been my observation that birth parents expect and deserve honesty. Also, birth parents who are already parenting children or are around children already know that child-rearing involves hardships, and information about the adoptee's life (a hitting phase, for example) will not come as a surprise.

Adoptive parents may choose to keep a running document of their child's developments, favorites, and experiences. This technique not only makes it easy to print, e-mail, or post, but it also helps the adoptive family keep a record of the child for themselves.

Photographs are particularly enjoyable to many birth parents. Send a variety including many of just the child. Professional pictures may also be appreciated. Though cell phones and social media websites make it easy for people to show off a photo of a child, many birth parents appreciate having hard copies of photos to look through at their leisure. Remember that photos sent via a cell phone or on a website can be shared beyond the adoptive family's control much more easily than can a hard copy.

Holidays

Holidays such as the child's birthday, Mother's or Father's Day, or Christmas can be particularly difficult for birth parents. Visits on or around these celebratory dates aren't always possible; however, adoptive parents and their children can create ways to bring the birth parents joy. A card or a small gift can be a nice surprise. A phone call or a text message can also be welcome.

One of my friends and fellow adoptive mother buys two of the same ornament each Christmas. She sends one to her daughter's birth mother and she hangs the other on their own family's Christmas tree. She chooses an ornament that reflects something significant in the child's life over the course of that year—a favorite or an accomplishment, for example.

It can be difficult to find cards that reflect the nature of your open adoption relationship. Cards tend to be written in categories such as for a parent or a friend. My suggestion is to buy a blank card and fill it with your own message. Young children can "sign" the card on the inside with a handprint traced by mom or dad. Older children can choose and sign the card themselves.

Homemade gifts are always special, as well. One year I embroidered our girls' handprints on a piece of cloth and framed them for their birth parents. Older children can draw pictures or create special art projects for birth parents.

Some adoptive families opt for store-bought gifts such as a special necklace featuring the child's birth stone, a journal, a Bible or inspirational book, a photo album, or a favorite item to support the birth parent's hobby or personality.

Gifts need not be elaborate or expensive. In any giving experience, it is the thought that truly counts the most.

First Parent? Birth Parent? First Name?

A complex question many adoptive parents face is about how they should refer to the birth parents when speaking with the adopted child. Like many facets of adoption, this is a highly personal decision that must take into account the level of the adoption's openness.

When speaking with the child, adoptive parents might choose from these options to refer to the birth parents:

- First name
- Miss, Ms., Mrs., or Mr. "First-name" or "Last-name," depending on the desired level of formality
- A nickname that the birth parent agrees to
- "Aunt" or "Uncle" followed by the first name

When speaking in terms of adoption in general, terms for a birth parent include:

- Birth parent
- Biological parent
- First parent
- Natural parent

Note that there are pros and cons to each term. Some of them can be considered archaic, offensive, or inaccurate; however, I provide them to demonstrate your range of options. Many adoptive parents and adoption professionals have strong feelings on what terminology is appropriate. But as with anything in adoption, one size doesn't fit all.

I do not suggest that birth parents be referred to as the child's "real" parents, as this can also confuse the child. (Young children tend to be quite literal in their thinking.) In many families, a child only knows one mother and one father, and qualifiers are used for additional people serving in mother or father roles such as "step-father" or "step-mother." Young children, especially, identify the primary caregiver as "mom" or "dad" (mama and dada are typically among a child's first words), so it can be confusing to a young child for you, as the primary caregiver, to encourage the child to call someone else, perhaps someone they rarely or never see, "mom" or "dad" (or a variation of these words).

On the other hand, adoptive parents should be prepared for the possibility that their child may change the name he or she uses to describe the birth parents as the child processes his or her feelings about the adoption and as the relationship with the birth parents evolves. As difficult as it might be to resist, some experts advise adoptive parents not to correct children who use a term that makes the adoptive parents uncomfortable. A child asking why her "real mom" couldn't keep her is likely not using "real" as a way to hurt the adoptive parents' feelings. Children gauge their parents' reactions to adoption questions; over-correcting your child (beyond for basic accuracy) may lead to the narrowing of adoption communication in the future.

In our home, we have chosen to refer to our girls' birth parents by their first names. When referring to them in a conversation with someone other than a close family members or close friend, we say "birth parent" to clarify whom we are speaking of and to protect their identity by not using their names publically.

Siblings

Some birth parents are parenting children, who are your child's biological siblings, and you have to decide how to refer to these children.

Some adoption experts believe that using the term "brother" or "sister" to refer to a sibling who is not in the same home as your child can be confusing to the child. This, of course, is true to a certain point. Older children can easily understand that two people don't have to live under the same roof to be siblings. Older children may also elect not to call their biological siblings "brother" or "sister."

Of course, just using the sibling's first name is probably the easiest option. When explaining the relationship, "half-birth-sister" might be a confusing term, whereas "your birth mom's daughter" might be easier for a child to understand.

Inevitably, your child will ask you why his or her birth parent is parenting other children but didn't "keep" him or her. Melina and Roszia share, "It is important for a child to hear that his birth parents could not take care of *any* baby born to them *at that time in their lives*. This communicates that it was the birth parents' situation, and not anything about the child, that was responsible for the placement" (248). A sibling may have arrived at a more practical time for parenting. This can be a difficult concept to explain to a child, depending on the child's age and maturity level, and parents are encouraged to seek professional support if necessary.

Questions from the Trenches

Strangers and even family members and friends are constantly asking me why my son's birth mother "gave him away" or "gave him up." This question, I feel, is really inappropriate, but I find myself giving a reason to satisfy their curiosity. I realize this can be detrimental to my son's privacy. What can I do?

The fact is, the idea that birth parents can place their children for adoption, no matter how dire the circumstances, is mind blowing. As adoptive parents, adoptive grandparents, friends, neighbors, even strangers, we see a precious child. So we wonder, *Why?*

You are absolutely right. The question is inappropriate. As an adoptive parent, I often want to say to someone who asks yet another intrusive question, "Just because you think something doesn't mean you have to say it!"

Karen J. Foli and John R. Thompson share in *The Post-Adoption Blues* that an adoptive parent (and argue that really, everyone) tends to "compare what decisions we would have made if we were faced with similar circumstances as the birthparent. Then we compare the similarities and differences. We try to empathize, to put ourselves in the other's place. What we are doing is trying to make sense of the birthparent's decision" (122-123). People ask because they are trying to figure out how a birth parent could do something so seemingly unnatural: give their child to someone else.

I have found that best way to respond, to protect your child's privacy as well as educate the asker, is to say, "Birth parents choose to place their children for adoption for any number of reasons. We are thankful to have our daughters, and we respect the decision their birth parents made." The exact reason for placement, whether you are privy to it or not, shouldn't be public information. If supplied, it will only be used to judge the birth parent's decision and to judge your child. Additionally, a specific answer will also encourage the person to ask more questions and delve deeper into your family's story.

Now, depending on your disclosure plan, you may choose (or not) to share the reason for placement with close relatives or friends—those your child might ask about the nature of his or her placement., But, at the minimum, tell them that if your child should ask this intimate question, they should tell the child to ask you instead so that you may disclose the information according to the child's age and maturity level.

I'm hurt and annoyed by the endless negative assumptions people make about my child's birth parents. I fear that these statements and questions will cloud my child's thus-far positive experience with open adoption. How should I respond to unfounded negative responses to our family's open relationship with our child's biological parents?

Highly-publicized and sensationalized adoption cases, such as those of Baby Richard and Baby Jessica, prompt the public (including your family members, friends, and strangers) to believe that your child's adoption is never fully final or legal. Likewise, movies such as *Like Dandelion Dust* and *Losing Isaiah* promote adoption stereotypes and often vilify the child's biological parents, making the public believe that all biological parents were unfit parents. Some commonly held stereotypes about birth parents include:

- They are young
- They are poor
- They abuse drugs or alcohol
- They are sexually promiscuous
- They are irresponsible and immature
- They don't love their children
- They are selfish
- They are incapable of parenting

In contrast, most popular media leads the public to believe that adoptive parents are saviors or heroes, wealthy, replacements for the child's biological parents, and always-fit parents. They are portrayed as free of addiction issues, mental illness, and immoral behaviors, as sexually abstinent or monogamous, as strongly religious, as infertile (the "victims" in an adoption situation), and as selfless saints who take in a child who "needs a good home."

It never ceases to amaze me how many people suddenly become self-designated social workers when the subject of adoption comes up. It's much like what happens when someone learns I'm a vegetarian. All the sudden, the person becomes a nutritionist and starts telling me how unhealthy and unnatural vegetarianism is. This demonstrates how powerful the media is for all of us. We think we know a lot about a subject because we've gained tidbits of insight (which is quite possibly inaccurate, biased, or outdated) through the media.

I always respond to open adoption and birth parent assumptions with education. If someone asks, "Are her birth parents young?" I say, "My adoption agency shared with me that most birth parents they serve are in their twenties." If a person asks, "Aren't you scared that your daughter's birth parents will show up on your front doorstep?", my response is, "I would let them into my house if they came to my front door. In fact, they know they have an open invitation to visit us at any time." Turning a potentially negative conversation into something productive and educational demonstrates to your child that you respect his or her privacy (by not disclosing specifics) and are not embarrassed that your family is part of an open adoption. Of course, you always have the option to simply say, "That's not up for discussion" or "We don't share that information outside of our immediate family."

I'm so tired of people referring to my child's birth parents as his "real mom" and "real dad." I am my son's real dad. How should I respond?

This is a common frustration among adoptive parents. It seems that the general public is uneducated about almost everything adoption-related, including terminology.

Adoptive parents approach this issue in many ways. Some say directly, "Do you mean my child's birth parent?" Or, "I am the child's real parent." Some might correct by saying, "Oh, you mean Jessica" (or whatever the birth parent's first name is).

If the offender is someone you see often or is a close family member or friend, consider speaking to them privately at some point. Something like, "I am sure you don't mean any harm, but when you refer to my son's birth parent as his 'real parent,' it confuses my son. Feel free to say 'birth parent' or just say her name."

In our case, if a person uses the phrase "her mom" or "her real mom" when referring to one of my girl's birth parents, I don't take offense. I know what the person means and understand that there is no malicious intent. I am secure in my role as my daughter's mother, and I don't see the need to correct someone unless my children are present.

I question whether an open adoption is the best decision for our family. The birth parents live a lifestyle and make decisions I don't approve of, and I fear this will somehow rub off on my child. Should we continue meeting for visits?

In *The Open Adoption Experience*, Lois Melina and Sharon Roszia write, "Sometimes the birth parents' behavior causes adoptive parents to reevaluate allowing their child to have contact with them. However, adoptive parents should consider that sometimes allowing the child to observe her birth parents' behavior directly can be an effective way to help the child understand why her birth parents could not raise a child" (237). However, she continues to say that sometimes the visits need to become "conditional." In other words, visits might need to take place in a neutral place and perhaps with supervision, such as by an adoption professional.

Some adoptive parents I have spoken with agreed to an open adoption out of ignorance (lack of education) or because they knew it would likely yield a quicker adoptive placement. If this is the case for you, it's not too late to start learning more about open adoption! It's also wise to reevaluate your open adoption agreement and make adjustments as needed.

You should also carefully evaluate why you desire a change in the open adoption agreement and whether adjustments are in the child's best interest. Is your grief resurfacing? Are insecurities clouding your judgment? Do you want to change the relationship based on personal discomfort or because there is a serious issue that could negatively affect your child? Seeking the help of an adoption professional might help. Open adoption can be confusing, and there is no shame in seeking assistance throughout the journey.

Of course, if the child's birth parents are acting inappropriately, you should, above all, do what is best for the child. After all, you are his or her parents. This might include speaking with the birth parents in private, possibly with the assistance of an adoption professional, and, if necessary, suspending the visits for a time until healthy boundaries are in place and are practiced.

Questions for Further Discussion

- What is my definition of open adoption?

- What are some of my fears surrounding open adoption? Are they based on fact, fiction, or just the unknown?

- What have I been taught to believe about biological parents by the media, by others, or by information I got elsewhere?

- Under what circumstances might I consider open adoption? Under what circumstances would open adoption not be an option I'd consider?

- How do I feel about the various levels of open adoption, and what kind of communication with birth parents would I consider participating in? Letters? Phone calls? Visits?

- What term will I use to refer to my child's biological parent(s)? What about any birth siblings?

Practical Application

Commit to reading one of the books suggested in the "Resources for Parents" list below to learn more about open adoption. Discuss any concerns or questions you have with an adoption professional. If possible, try to connect with some biological parents who are participating in an open adoption to get their perspective.

Resources for Parents

Antwone Fisher (DVD)

August Rush (DVD)

Beverly Lewis' The Shunning (DVD)

Dear Birthmother (Kathleen Silber)

Jessica Lost: A Story of Birth, Adoption, & The Meaning of Motherhood (Bunny Crumpacker and J.S. Picariello)

Like Dandelion Dust (DVD)

The Duchess (DVD)

The Girls Who Went Away (Ann Fessler)

The Language of Flowers (Vanessa Diffenbaugh)

The Light Between Oceans (M.L. Stedman)

The Shunning, The Confession, and The Reckoning (Beverly Lewis)

The Open Adoption Experience (Lois Ruskai Melina and Sharon Kaplan Roszia)

Where We Belong (Emily Giffin)

Without a Map (Meredith Hall)

Resources for Kids

Megan's Birthday Tree (Laurie Lears)

Mommy Far, Mommy Near: An Adoption Story (Carol Antoinette Peacock)

Motherbridge of Love (Xinran)

Penguin and Pinecone (Salina Yoon)

The Tummy Mummy (Michelle Madrid-Branch)

CHAPTER SEVEN

Processing, Talking About, and Confronting Racism: From the N-Word to Watermelon

"Hatred paralyzes life; love releases it. Hatred confuses life; love harmonizes it. Hatred darkens life; love illuminates it."

~Dr. Martin Luther King Jr.

"The only tired I was, was tired of giving in."

~Rosa Parks, on refusing to give up her bus seat to a White man

I recently had a conversation with a friend and fellow adoptive mother about letting grandparents babysit the kids. She said that her parents hadn't cared for a young child since she was a baby and that they seemed to forget how children can walk into a room and immediately (and quite sneakily) find danger: an uncovered outlet, a slightly open patio door, a forgotten pair of scissors. She then said, "I can walk into a room and know, immediately, what the dangers are and which ones my child will attempt to handle."

Similarly, transracial adoptive families quickly learn to be aware of and spot problematic people and situations.

I don't want my children to be fearful that everyone is judging them, and I don't want them to feel that humans cannot be great, trustworthy, loving people. Yet I have to prepare them for the reality: not everyone is going to think they are as fabulous as we do. They will be judged for not only being adopted, but also for being transracially adopted, and for simply being Black. Judgment will come from people of many races (not just Blacks or just Whites), ages, generations, and so on.

What is racism, exactly? What forms of racism might a family or an adoptee encounter? How can parents prepare their child for racist encounters, and what can parents do when a racist incident occurs? The answers to these questions, and so much more, will be addressed in this chapter.

Things I Often Hear White People Say

- "Race doesn't matter."

- "I am colorblind. I couldn't care less if someone is white, black, purple, or green."

- "I'm not racist. I have a friend who is Black."

- "Why is there a Black History Month? Shouldn't there be a White History Month too?"

- "Why is it OK for a Black person to call another Black person a nigger?"

- "Talking about skin color puts too much emphasis on race."

- "I don't understand why everyone says that President Obama is our first Black president. He's White *and* Black."

- "The world is a melting pot."

- "I'm so tired of people playing the race card. Slavery and civil rights times are over. It's time for them to take responsibility for their actions."

- "Don't worry about teaching your kids about race. They are too young to understand or care. And by the time they are older, racism will be a thing of the past."

Transracial adoptive parents often fear the typical racist portrayed in movies: the middle-aged White man who refers to Black people as niggers and flies a Confederate flag off his front porch. But the racism many people of color encounter is not from the stereotypical racist. Instead, it comes from those they encounter in everyday life: a family member, a friend, a neighbor, a teacher, a cashier at the grocery store, a police officer.

If you believe that the world is generally colorblind and that we are "beyond" race, I am here to tell you that it is not the case. Further, we like to believe in degrees of racism, but the truth is that racism is racism, especially when it comes to the safety and well-being of your child. Parents have a duty to evaluate the damaging effects racism can have on a child and on the entire family.

Jayne E. Schooler and Thomas C. Atwood, authors of *The Whole Life Adoption Book: Realistic Advice for Building A Healthy Adoptive Family*, write of adopted children that they "need to know that parents are on their side if insensitive or insulting comments come not from other children but from adults, even adults within their own extended families. While some family members may possess certain reservations about transcultural adoption and its real and perceived challenges, often this uneasiness or fear melts away as soon as the adopted child is introduced to the family. However, in some cases extended family members or close friends may never come to fully understand or accept the adoption" (69).

The Many Faces of Racism

Racism can present itself in a variety of ways. Some examples of racism are:

- A racist joke

- A stereotype ("Blacks like watermelon and fried chicken" or "Blacks are inherently great dancers and good basketball players")

- Name-calling ("nigger," "colored," "ghetto," "monkey," etc.)

- Avoidance of someone because of skin color (in other words, the idea that Blacks are suspicious or scary simply because they have brown skin)

- Someone not being believed due to being darker-skinned (the media grossly underreports missing Black children compared to missing light-skinned children; some believe that when a Black child goes missing the parent is at fault, while White children are assumed to be victims of a malicious crime, such as a kidnapping by a child predator)

- Someone being closely attended because of skin color (such as when a Black teen is followed by a security cop in a mall, despite the teen's proper conduct, or when Black athletes and music artists are given ample media attention while Black writers, government leaders, filmmakers, and scientists receive little, thus enforcing racial stereotypes and ignoring Blacks in intellectual, governmental, and other fields)

- Someone being selected due to skin color (being called upon by a teacher to give an answer that is expected to represent the views of the entire Black race)

Real World Examples

Unless someone has personally experienced racism—either through a single, memorable incident, or repeated, it's difficult for him or her to believe that racism still exists today. As stated earlier, many Whites are eager to preach "colorblindness," "world peace," and "harmony" among races. This is because Whites have long been the dominant race in society and experience White privilege, though they are often unaware of it. Many believe that talking about and teaching about race only emphasizes differences; however, I argue that history makes all people who they are today and that ignoring history does a disservice to those who fought for equality—sometimes laying down their lives for the greater good of all people. Furthermore, transracial adoptive parents who wish to raise confident and successful children do not have the luxury of ignoring reality.

The following are relevant, current examples of racism, in various degrees:

- CBS News reported in July of 2012 that Charles and Te'Andrea Wilson were told, the day before their scheduled wedding, that they couldn't marry at the First Baptist Church in Crystal Springs, Mississippi, because they were Black. A small number of vocal congregants spoke out against the couple marrying in the church, so the pastor chose to marry the couple elsewhere to avoid further conflict within the church and with the couple.

- Missing Blacks are grossly underreported by local and national media, while cases of missing Whites—especially White children—receive national attention. Missing White females tend to get the most media: Natalie Holloway, Jaycee Duggard, Caylee Anthony, Lisa Irwin, Laci Peterson. (The Black and Missing Foundation attempts to combat this issue by bringing more attention to missing Blacks.)

- In early 2012, ABC News reported that Beaver Ridge Elementary school in Norcross, Georgia assigned some of its students a math homework assignment that included questions such as, "If Frederick got two beatings per day, how many beatings did he get in one week?" and "Each tree had 56 oranges. If eight slaves pick them equally, how much will each slave pick?" The teachers who wrote and distributed the homework assignment claim they were attempting to combine two subjects: social studies and math. ABC News noted that "The assignment outraged parents, community activists and members of the Georgia NAACP."

- Overwhelmingly, Black characters are only sidekicks to White leads in movies, television shows, and even in cartoons. Hollywood passes Black issues and Black history over in favor of White-focused films. Though some television shows hint that their Black actors are co-stars, oftentimes such actors are presented as racially ambiguous, like Maya Rudolph as Ava in the television show *Up All Night* or Rashida Jones in *Parks and Recreation*. According to CNN. com, Kerry Washington, a Black actor, plays a lead role on a major network television show (*Scandal*) for the first time in thirty-eight years. In sixteen seasons of ABC's hit show *The Bachelor*, there has never been a non-White star, as reported by Entertainment Weekly website. Blacks continue to be underrepresented in advertisements, magazine covers, and greeting cards, as well. And when Blacks are featured, they are almost always light-skinned. According to USA Today's website, George Lucas, director of epic films such as *Star Wars* and *Indiana Jones*, was rejected time and time again by Hollywood executives when he presented *Red Tails*, a film that focuses on the Tuskegee airmen, to them. The film was allegedly rejected due to its all-Black cast. Lucas chose to fund the film himself.

- In June 2012, MSN reported that allegedly "Kathleen Pyles, a math teacher at North End Middle School in Waterbury,

Conn., became agitated when the student corrected her when she called him the wrong name, reportedly responding, 'How about black boy? Go sit down, black boy.'"

- There is only one national holiday honoring a Black leader, Dr. Martin Luther King Jr.'s birthday. There are no additional national holidays honoring a non-White person (or a woman).

- White skin is the standard by which the color of many products is calibrated, including "flesh" colored bandages and "skin-tone" ballet tights.

- There continues to be a dearth of Black dolls and action figures. And often, even when Black dolls and action figures feature brown skin, their other features are that of a typical White person (such as green or blue eyes and blond or light brown hair).

Discussing and Dealing With Racism

Introducing a child to words like "racism," "discrimination," and "prejudice" can be incredibly daunting for parents, and sometimes families avoid discussing race at all because it's simply too complicated and uncomfortable. However, Black children, including transracially adopted children, will inevitably face racism, discrimination, and prejudice. Parents should be first in line to prepare and discuss these issues with their children.

Using a book, a film, or a personal experience, parents can introduce basic definitions to children. For example, when my oldest daughter was three, she loved reading about Rosa Parks because she had an infatuation with all-things transportation, including buses. So I used her interest in buses to introduce her to Rosa Parks. We talk about how some people don't like other people because of the color of their skin, and we discuss how Rosa stood up for herself and other people who looked like her.

Note that the main message in our discussions is that there are many people who stand up for what is right and that they are brave, strong, and honest. Parents of young Black children shouldn't "Unnecessarily burden them with knowledge of society's pervasive racism. These parents believe that they are preparing their children to deal with reality, but for young children, knowledge that is thrust upon them too soon may have the opposite effect: it may make them feel that their skin color is such an overwhelming handicap that they can never transcend it" (Wright 64-65). See chapter 9 for explanations on a child's understanding of race based on age.

Obviously, adoptive parents do not want to overly emphasize race and racism; however, a parent's willingness to discuss difficult subjects demonstrates that when an incident does occur (as it will at some point), that the lines of communication are open, honesty is welcomed and encouraged, and the family will work together to face difficult situations.

Betsy Keefer and Jayne E. Schooler, authors of *Telling the Truth to Your Adopted or Foster Child: Making Sense of the Past*, offer these tips on how parents can discuss race and racism with their children:

- "Listen more; Talk less." The authors state, "As the authorities in the family, parents often feel that they are appropriately providing guidance and instruction for their children only when they are doing the talking. Yet all effective leaders and teacher have learned the art of listening. Before teaching and guiding, parents must first understand where the child is in his experience, perception, and development" (147).

- "Ask open-ended questions." "To understand the child's perceptions, parents should not ask questions that can be answered with a monosyllable" (148).

- "Don't turn into a psychological dentist, extracting feelings as if they were bad teeth." "Parents should not constantly search for the horizon for racial or cultural problems that do not exist for the child. It is possible to *over*respond to the racial and cultural issues faced by adopted and foster children" (148).

- "Create a code word or gesture for dealing with rude remarks in public." "When strangers or casual acquaintance make ridiculously rude remarks in the presence of the child, many families find it helpful to communicate their desire to terminate the encounter through the use of a secret code word or gesture" (148).

What should a parent do when the child reports a racist incident? Schooler and Atwood, authors of *The Whole Life Adoption Book: Realistic Advice for Building a Healthy Adoptive Family*, encourage parents to do the following (68-69):

- *"Don't overreact or rush out to confront the offender.* You cannot act without the facts, and if you are busy leaping to your child's immediate defense or fighting his battles for him, then you are not listening to his story or sharing in his pain."

- *"Ask the child to explain to you exactly what happened without leaving anything out.* While an insult may have been clearly intended, it may also have been accidental. Either way, the child's feelings are legitimate, but it's important for her to be able to tell you the entire story so you know exactly what happened and she knows you are there to listen."

- *"Encourage the child to tell you how he felt.* Ask him to use descriptive terms and be specific: 'I felt angry; I felt scared; I felt sad; I felt embarrassed; I felt lonely.'"

- *"Ask what the child said in reply.* She may not have responded, but if she did and the situation was handled well, you can praise her for her maturity and quick thinking."

- *"Ask the child to consider how he might handle it differently in the future.* Your child may have doubts about how he handled the situation. Explain to him that he does have choices in how he fields questions or rude remarks about his race, culture, or adoption. If he has trouble coming up with possible options for future encounters, help him identify some alternatives."

The authors also share, "Parents should also ask their child whether or not he or she wants you to do anything about the situation. While most children will not want direct parental involvement, it will help them know that the possibility exists and that their parents are on their side" (69).

The authors of *White Parents, Black Children* suggest that if you decide to address the issue, keep in mind that in some cases, you might be accused of: "reverse racism, exaggeration, overreacting, and 'playing the race card'" (106). The authors warn White parents to avoid "Framing the [racist] event as a personal momentary failing" on someone's part instead of "framing the incident as racial" when it *is* racial. Adoptive parents must not minimize "the consequences of racial mistreatment in order to get along with Whites" (107). Despite resistance you might encounter from whoever the higher-ups are in the situation—say your child's teacher (per an example provided in the book)—White parents need to stay in touch with their intuition. If a situation presents itself as racist, it probably is. To defer to the "White goodness and racial innocence" (107) that social privilege tends to impute to the racist party is to undermine your child's needs and teach him or her that White people, particularly those in authoritative positions, should be given a free pass. Remember, your obligation is to your child, not to the feelings of anyone else, including a White person in a powerful position.

The term "racism" or "racist" puts people on the defense, as most people prefer not to be labeled as such. Carefully consider how you will address the situation to achieve the desired result; however, don't shy away from being blatantly honest. Avoid name-calling; focus on the incident and what your suggested resolution is.

Parental Checkup

Marguerite A. Wright, author of *I'm Chocolate, You're Vanilla: Raising Healthy Black and Biracial Children in a Race-Conscious World*, offers a list of suggestions for parents of bi-racial and Black children, including (74, 77, 78):

- "Be brief." When a child asks a question, make sure your answer responds to the question honestly and directly. Lengthy, complex answers confuse children, especially young children.

- "Avoid harmful stereotyping." "Racism is just one of the many isms (including sexism, ageism, chauvinism, and lookism) that seeks to rob people of their inherent human dignity."

- "Focus on developing your child's character and talents." "The child who learns to be thoughtful regarding others and develops her social and intellectual abilities has a better chance at having a happy childhood than one who focuses on her appearance."

- "Provide the basics." "Children who are raised in a nurturing environment where they feel loved, supported, and valued have the best chance of developing a healthy self-image. [...] How can children feel positive racial esteem when they do not even feel positive personal esteem?"

Again, using supportive materials such as films and books, as well as incorporating racial role models into racial discussions, can assist you in discussing race and dealing with racism.

Questions from the Trenches

I'm preparing to adopt transracially, and I'm fearful of being placed with a Black boy. It seems that Black males are marginalized in society more than any other race or sex. For this reason, I'm tempted to adopt a girl.

Black males are among the most "unadoptable" children in society. Look at any website that lists waiting children and you will see that many of them are older, Black males and sibling groups that include all or several Black males. Why this is, exactly, probably comes down to a myriad of factors including the media's presentation of Black males (as criminals and players, for example) and frequently shared statistics on the number of Black male high school drop outs, prisoners, and violent offenders.

Parenting Black males is different, I believe, from parenting Black females. After Trayvon Martin's death, a slew of articles were published on the topic of preparing Black males for the real world: a world where Black males face an incredible amount of prejudice. Many authors noted that they have taught their Black sons always to do exactly as police officers ask, never to go sprinting down a street or sidewalk (for fear that people and police will assume they are committing a crime), and to speak respectfully to all persons of authority such as teachers, law enforcement, and bosses. Other authors commented that they have taught their sons to dress "respectably" (no sagging pants, oversized t-shirts, or hoodie sweatshirts) so they appear to be trustworthy to those they encounter.

Parents face a wide range of choices and decisions when it comes to what type of child (sex, age, race, ability) they are open to adopting. Arguably, deciding what one is really open to is the toughest task the waiting adoptive parent faces.

As with anything in adoption, education helps you make the best decision for your family. As discussed in other chapters, you also want to consider where you live, what your support system is like, and what changes, if any, you are willing to make to best prepare for any child of color — male or female.

Children's clothing lines seem to feature animals, such as monkeys, and fruits, such as watermelons. Though these outfits are cute, I am afraid to put such clothing on my Black children for fear that they enforce stereotypes. Am I being oversensitive?

This is a discussion I had with other transracial adoptive parents early in our adoption journey. At what point do we stop worrying too much about racial stereotypes and just let kids be kids?

Take, for example, friends of ours who adopted a Black male. One afternoon while we were visiting them, my friend pulled me into the hallway and told me she had redecorated her son's bathroom. She then turned on the light to show me its jungle-theme, complete with a monkey-and-banana printed shower curtain, rug, and towels. She shared about how she hadn't been sure she wanted to go with the jungle-theme her son was interested in because of the old "Blacks are like monkeys" insults. But in the end, she went with what pleased her son.

I used to be much more sensitive to such instances, I think in the name of being the transracial adoptive "super-parent." I didn't want to appear to be unknowledgeable about race. But as my children grew older, they began, as all children do, to develop preferences. For example, my daughters love the television show *Curious George*. Would I forbid them to watch the program or wear a Curious George t-shirt due to what I see as an overprotective racial awareness?

Children shouldn't be unnecessarily burdened with racial issues. When situations arise, yes, they should be addressed, and yes, children should be prepared to a proper degree. They will have to know that racial prejudice will occur and that they will have to be ready to combat it. However, adoptive parents can go too far. Forbidding children to consume watermelon and fried chicken or refusing to let them play with a stuffed monkey will only make them hyper-sensitive about race.

Though your intentions are noble, acting on them will likely do far more harm than good.

How am I supposed to explain words like "cracker" and "nigger" to my child? The conversation hasn't come up yet, but I know it's coming. Should I bring these words up to my child before he or she hears them, or should I wait until my child asks?

When I was in grade school, my family and I were watching a series of television shows on a Friday night, including *Family Matters*, a show featuring a Black family. In one episode, Laura, one of the characters, was walking through the hallway at her school and saw the word "nigger" spray-painted across a locker. The background music, the close-up shot of the locker, and the gasps of Laura's peers told me that the word meant something terrible. I don't recall the discussion I had with my parents after the show, but I do remember watching it quite vividly.

I suggest you refer to the age-by-age guide in chapter 9, using that as a starting point to decide when certain racial discussions should happen with your child. If an opportunity presents itself (such as one prompted by a TV show), you can explain to your child what a certain word means as you deem appropriate. Using supporting materials, such as books, films, or discussions with racial role models, may also be helpful.

Talking about race is much like talking about sex. It's inevitable that the topic will come up, but your child might only bring it up once or twice (or never!). It's up to you as parents to take initiative to discuss such crucial topics and to reintroduce and continue such discussions when necessary. Children shouldn't be burdened with the responsibility of initiating important discussions, because for one thing, they are children, and for another, depending on the child's personality and level of comfort, the discussion may never come about.

Also, carefully monitor what your child is reading, watching, and listening to. Make sure that the child is engaging with appropriate materials. You can't be with the child at all times, moderating all conversations and media, but you can establish that you are going to bring up important topics with your child and that you are always willing to engage in discussions (openly, honestly, and not overly emotionally) with your child.

I have a family member who just doesn't understand why we aren't going to adopt a child who shares our race. I understand this person grew up in a time when races "didn't mix." I'm not sure how to respond in a manner that is productive and loving.

I do understand how difficult it is to change one's long-held beliefs. When a person hasn't had any experiences with people of other races or hasn't invested in learning about the benefits and joys of adopting transracially, it's quite challenging for them to grasp how your decision could possibly be successful, happy, and "right."

I have received e-mails from blog readers stating how discouraged they are when a family member protests against the parent's decision to adopt transracially. Those we love the most hurt us the most with their judgments.

First, remember that if it comes down to it, you must choose your child over your family member. When you take on the role of mom or dad, your allegiance must always be to your child. But before you start thinking too much about cutting the family member out of your life for good, consider how you can help. Offer resources to the family member: books, articles, films, support groups. And offer to engage in respectful discussions about race with the person. It's likely that race has been either a very hateful or quite taboo topic in the person's life; therefore, offer the opportunity to have productive and honest conversations.

Finally, a change of heart may come about once the child arrives. Talking about race and thinking about race are quite different from engaging with an innocent child who happens to be of another race. While some might label a person in terms of skin color, engaging with the child, learning his or her personality, playing with the child, and seeing how it is possible for the child to help complete a family, might be what it takes to change the family member's heart and mind.

Questions for Further Discussion

- What statements have you encountered about race that you have found to be untrue based on your transracial parenting experiences?

- How do you respond when someone makes a statement about race that you believe to be inaccurate or inappropriate?

- Think about racist incidents your family has encountered and how you have responded. What would be more effective responses?

- What resources have you found to be effective in talking to your child about racism? What resources could you add to your home library for future discussions?

- What reservations do you have about adopting and raising a Black female? A Black male? Or, what have you observed along your parenting journey when it comes to parenting a Black male versus a Black female?

Practical Application

As a family, use books, videos, music, museum and monument visits, and other resources to learn more about a Black leader who dealt with discrimination. Talk to your children about how they might model their responses to discrimination after the behavior of a respected Black leader. For example, my oldest daughter enjoyed learning about how Ruby Bridges chose to respond to those who yelled at her as she entered a previously all-White school by continuing to walk and by praying for those who persecuted her.

Resources for Parents

Everyday Antiracism: Getting Real About Race in School (Mica Pollock)

Letters Across the Divide: Two Friends Explore Racism, Friendship, and Faith (David Anderson and Brent Zuercher)

Other People's Children: Cultural Conflict in the Classroom (Lisa Delpit)

Racism: A Short History (George M. Frederickson)

Racism Explained to My Daughter (Tahar Ben Jelloun)

Racism without Racists: Color-Blind Racism and the Persistence of Racial Inequality in America (Eduardo Bonilla-Silva)

Silent Racism: How Well-Meaning White People Perpetuate the Racial Divide (Barbara Trepagnier)

The New Jim Crow (Michelle Alexander)

Uprooting Racism: How White People Can Work for Racial Justice (Paul Kivel)

"Why Are All The Black Kids Sitting Together in the Cafeteria?" And Other Conversations About Race (Beverly Daniel Tatum)

www.tolerance.org

Resources for Kids

Black Like Kyra, White Like Me (Judith Vigna)

No Two Alike (Keith Baker)

Pretzel (Margaret Rey)

The Absolutely True Diary of a Part-Time Indian (Sherman Alexie)

The Other Side (Jacqueline Woodson)

The Skin I'm In: A First Look at Racism (Pat Thomas)

The Sneetches and Other Stories (Dr. Seuss)

To Be Free: Understanding and Eliminating Racism (Thomas D. Peacock and Marlene Wisuri)

What If the Zebras Lost Their Stripes? (John Reitano)

White Water (Michael S. Bandy and Eric Stein)

CHAPTER EIGHT

It Takes a Village: Creating Support

"A man who isolates himself seeks his own desire;
He rages against all wise judgment."

~PROVERBS 18:1

"There is a comfortable anonymity to blending into one's
surroundings. Children and adults feel a constant, low level
of stress by being the only person of a particular race in their
school, on their street, or in the grocery store. Even if they
are 'accepted,' the word itself points out the difference factor.
Someone else has the choice of accepting or not accepting. In
their making the choice, often the naturalness of an everyday
interaction is changed."

~ DEBORAH D. GRAY, ATTACHING IN ADOPTION

Adoption and transracial parenting, as we have established, is a unique journey—one that isn't, I believe, meant to be traveled alone. Though the journey can be isolating at times, it's crucial that you consistently connect with those who are in the trenches alongside you.

Transracial adoption, adoption in general, and parenting adopted children is isolating for many reasons, including that:

- Your child wasn't born to you.

- Your child doesn't share your race or other physical features.

- Your child has two sets of parents, and whether the other set is involved or not, there will always be challenges.

- Your child came to you with a history, sometimes a traumatic one.

- Your child may have a disability, disease, or condition.

- You likely adopted due to a loss that others in your family and circle of friends haven't had to face.

- You are frequently reminded that your family is different.

- You face adoptism.

- You face racism.

I'm in my thirties, a season of life during which many people are having children—sometimes several. At any given time, a number of my friends are expecting a baby, so naturally, their conversations, their struggles, and their Facebook posts tend to center on their experiences. Get-togethers with friends often yield conversations about childbirth, breastfeeding, pregnancy weight gain, cravings, and stretch marks. Though I can throw in a comment here or there about nighttime feedings, potty training adventures, and first words, many of my friends' favorite topics of conversation are foreign to me.

Adoptive parents need to have a support system in place, one that addresses the unique challenges and joys of adoption. This is where they can commune with like-minded and like-experienced individuals on topics of reactive attachment disorder (RAD), relationships with birth parents, and responding to comments and questions from strangers.

Same-race adoptive families need support too, but transracial adoptive families have an even greater need because they can't go anywhere without the adoptive family's status being obvious and often mentioned. There is no concealing it.

Seeking Support

There are many avenues through which transracial adoptive families can create a support system:

- *Join an existing transracial adoptive parent support group.* Your support group might meet online or in person. If you live in a populated area, there may be multiple groups to choose from. Attend a few meetings to determine whether a group is the right fit for you before committing your time and energy to its events, especially if there is a financial commitment. If children are involved in group meetings, you'll want to make sure your kids are comfortable with being part of the group and that topics discussed and activities are age and maturity-level appropriate.

- *Start a support group.* This is what I did. All the groups in my area were country-specific (Ethiopian adoption, Chinese adoption, etc.). I asked a few adoptive families from my church if they'd like to join me in a new group, and three years later, my group has evolved into an adoptive mother support group of almost forty. The women in my group have adopted domestically, internationally, and through foster care; some have adopted family members. My group is not is not limited to those who adopt transracially; the variety of women who attend helps me be a better adoptive parent.

- *Befriend other transracial adoptive families.* Initially, this might be difficult, but take the step. If you see another adoptive family, approach them. I have done this many times, and the vast majority of my introductions have been warmly received. Don't limit yourself to adoptive families, necessarily. You can seek friendships with multi-racial families as well, who likely experience many of the challenges with race that your own family faces.

- *Find a mentor.* Once you are a member of a support group and you have other adoptive families as friends, ask someone to mentor you — preferably a well-seasoned adoptive parent. This person should be trustworthy, knowledgeable, understanding, and encouraging.

- *Join in on community events.* Attend local cultural celebrations such as festivals, concerts, food tastings, and so on to meet new people and learn more about your child's culture and other cultures. You need not limit these outings to those that are particular to your family's racial makeup. Teaching your children about other cultures and their traditions is important, too.

- *Touch base with your social worker.* This person likely has experience gathered from working with many adoptive families and can offer guidance and support. He or she might also be able to point you to additional resources, support groups, and online web forums.

Change is Good

Adoptive families benefit from evaluating their decisions from time to time to determine whether they are, within their means and circumstances, making the best choices for their transracially adopted children.

Evaluate the diversity of each of these places, groups, or establishments. (Consider that diversity is not just racial; it can include age, sex, ability, socioeconomic status, etc., but racial diversity, of course, is especially important to transracial adoptive families.)

- Your county, city or town, and neighborhood
- Your place of worship
- Your place of employment
- Your friends
- Groups you and your child belong to: clubs, sports, committees, classes, etc.
- Your child's school or future school (including the student population, teaching staff, and administration)
- Your family's health care team: dentist, doctor, therapist, etc.
- Your go-to restaurants, grocery stores, gyms, shops, etc.

Once you examine these environments, consider where you might make changes that can to expose your family to more diversity and create more opportunities for friendships and support. Obviously making changes in some of these areas might be more difficult than in others, such as switching jobs or moving. However, when you see an opportunity (or better yet, actively seek change in these areas), assess the diversity you experience now and ask yourself how you might improve upon it.

For example, my family lived in a racially diverse community; however, our school district was not stellar. As a college teacher, I see the effects a mediocre education has on a student. It was very important to my family that our daughters receive an excellent education. Private school wasn't an option for us, as the private schools in our area consist overwhelmingly and predominately of White middle-to-upper class students. Therefore, we made the decision to move to a new town that was in a better school district, though it is not quite as racially diverse as our previous town. However, we also knew that we would have continued opportunities to attend cultural community events, travel, enjoy our favorite soul food restaurant, and work in our same diverse places of employment. It was a difficult decision and one we didn't take lightly, but we made it in confidence knowing that we had done our research and had thought through the many benefits and drawbacks.

Other decisions you face are less dramatic. For example, say your family goes out to dinner a few times a month. Maybe you go to your usual places, but after reflection, you realize they aren't very racially diverse. The patrons, the servers, the managers — the majority are White and the food is equally monochromatic: burgers, fries, and soda. So you decide, as our family did, that a few times a year you'll travel farther to have dinner somewhere else, like a soul food restaurant. Again, you don't have to limit your choices to those rooted in your child's racial culture. One day my daughter saw a television show about Japanese food. She asked if she could try it, and I agreed that we should. Trying new places gives you and your child exposure to new experiences and people. You will develop a greater appreciation for diversity and your child will see your willingness and openness to it.

Perhaps you have already taken a few steps. Despite living in a majority-White community, you have chosen a Black pediatrician. Though this step is commendable (as long as the doctor is a good fit for your family), it's likely your child doesn't see the doctor all that often.

Consider, for a moment, a family who rarely spends any time together. Mom and Dad are both working fifty-hour-a-week jobs. The oldest child is in three after-school activities that consume not only every week-night, but also all day Saturdays and Sundays. The younger child attends preschool, going directly after school to the babysitter's house until about seven o'clock every night. Dad picks up the younger child, brings her home, and plops her in front of cartoons so he can relax for a few minutes. Meanwhile, Mom brings the older child home from karate class and then hands out a bagged, fast-food meal to the family.

Mom and Dad feel guilty for being so busy, so they commit to taking a family vacation. They'll take off a week of work and take the family to Disney World. They plan excursions, special meals eaten alongside costumed characters, attend parades, and enjoy various rides. The family has a wonderful trip. They return home on a Sunday afternoon, and on Monday, they resume their normal activities until Mom and Dad plan the next vacation a few years later.

Though the parents' intentions were good and they invested time, money, and energy into their children, the one-week event is such a small part of the kids' childhoods. It may be enjoyable, but a seven-day trip doesn't make up for the other fifty-one weeks of sheer busyness and the lack of peace and downtime with the family.

Incorporating diversity into your family's life can either be a few-times-in-eighteen-years Disney trip, or it can be a frequent or even everyday occurrence. Though it can be hard to see how the seemingly insignificant decisions to choose one restaurant over another or select one neighborhood to move to versus a different one, these decisions can establish a continuance of diversity in your family's life.

Why Is Diversity So Important?

We hear a lot about diversity, but what does it really mean, and why is it important?

Diversity simply means "variation." Many adoptive parents ask, "Is promoting and exposing my family to diversity putting an over-emphasis on difference? Won't this do more harm than good in my child's life?"

Consider this: a lack of similarity among people is just a different kind of similarity. Adoptive parents can help their children feel less isolated (which can be especially prevalent among transracial adoptees who experience multiple forms of prejudice) and more assimilated and accepted by exposing the children to different "types" of people. Remember, transracial adoptees have the cards stacked against them in the sense that they are seen as different from the "normal" son or daughter in a traditional family, plus they don't racially match their parent(s) — which means that their adoption is obvious, and racial tensions are raised by the simple fact that the adoptive family exists and is visible.

The fact is your child needs to be exposed to diversity to understand that he or she isn't alone in being different. There are all kinds of people, and the fact that everyone is different (some in more obvious ways than others), means that there is a common thread among humans that can help adoptees build relationships with others and establish self-worth, self-awareness, and racial identity.

Friendships

Again, diversity isn't limited to race. Consider the importance of your child seeing friendships you have with people of different ages. I have friends who are grandmothers, and I have friends who are in their early twenties. I have friends who have many children, and I have childless friends. Some of my friends share my religious faith while others do not. Granted, I didn't necessarily seek out this variety of friends; however, life lead me to these individuals who love, support, care for, and advise me.

Many adoptive parents think: "What am I supposed to do? Specifically target people of my child's race and try desperately to befriend them just to benefit my child? Isn't that racist in some way? The whole idea makes me uncomfortable."

The answer is: yes and no. By choosing to adopt transracially, adoptive parents have chosen a path that requires more than what is expected of non-adoptive families to be successful. Diversity is especially important to the transracial adoptive family. However, I will argue that the parents of a biological, same-race family shouldn't shirk responsibility here either. Exposure to diversity is important for every person, not just the transracial adoptee, so that all children can grow up to be appreciative of, understanding of, and friendly with a diverse group of people. It is especially important for preparing children to be productive adults who will likely study and eventually work with a variety of people.

Children have a keen ability to understanding that adults sometimes forget, ignore, or are unaware of. Children are always learning how to react to circumstances by watching their parents. If children see that their parents are approachable and open to making new friends of all kinds, children will learn that this is an acceptable (or even desirable) behavior.

I have learned that setting my pride and insecurities aside is a powerful way to make transracial adoptive parenting successful. For example, we recently moved into a new house within walking distance of a beautiful park. When the weather is nice, we walk to the park and play. On several occasions, despite my initial reservations about walking up to strangers, my girls and I have approached people of my girls' race to say hi and chat. Once, I met the assistant principal of a local school. As my daughters played with hers, the woman gave me her phone number so our girls could play together some time.

Meeting new people can be intimidating, especially when the adoptive parent is nervous about approaching a person of his or her child's race. The reservation might come from a personal lack of exposure to adults of the child's race, a negative past experience with brown-skinned adults, or simply a nervousness that comes from the fear of being judged as a transracial adoptive parent. There is always a possibility that the people you approach will judge you, reject you, ignore you, or insult you. But I have found that overwhelmingly, the adoptive parent who makes the effort to be friendly receives a warm welcome. Friendships cannot be formed unless someone takes the first step and says a simple hello.

Granted, I'm not going to befriend someone I have no connection with, even if they are of my child's race. Friendships are built on the basis of some sort of commonality. Not all encounters that you have—maybe not even most of them—are going to result in a long-term friendship. However, again it's important to remember that unless you act, you could be denying yourself even the opportunity to make new friendships with people of your child's race.

Once you become closer to a person of your child's race, it's fair to predict that both of you will share more intimate details about your lives. I recall a time in my parenting journey when I began to question whether I was doing enough to expose my children to same-race role models. Finding myself in a state of panic, I approached a woman with whom I took an exercise class a few times a week. I asked her if we could go out to lunch. She said yes, so the following week we met at a local café.

I admit, I was quite nervous. I didn't want this woman to feel that I had targeted her because she was Black and expected her to act as a representative for the entire race. I did feel that I desperately needed her wisdom and advice, since she was brown-skinned like my children.

Much to my relief, she was extraordinarily helpful and receptive to my concerns. She listened attentively and responded honestly. She shared some of her story with me. The most beautiful part of the conversation was when she complimented my parenting. As a White woman, I have faced some scrutiny from members of the Black community for adopting Black children and accused of stealing "their" babies away. However, I had to set aside these past comments, squelch my pride and fear, and embrace the possibility that our lunch meeting would enhance my understanding of transracial parenting. It did.

Racial Role Models

There are many successful and honorable Black Americans my children can "look up to." These individuals range from American heroes past such as Rosa Parks, Martin Luther King Jr., Jackie Robinson, and Ella Fitzgerald (who has the same first name as my oldest) to modern day figures such as Barack and Michelle Obama, Venus and Serena Williams, Oprah Winfrey, and Reverend T.D. Jakes. I love teaching my children about people such as these who have risen above adversity and who offer the possibility of success to younger generations.

However, I will say again that in the day-to-day raising of transracially adopted children, such "celebrities" are not within reach. They might grace magazine covers, be the subject of chapters in history books or children's biographical titles, or be featured on a television show, but they are not standing beside adoptive parents offering advice and support and encouragement. They aren't walking your child to school or speaking at their Scout meetings.

Consistent and positive interactions between your family and people of your child's race are important. A child needs to see that the media need not be the only teacher about race. We know that movies and television shows rarely star people of color. Brown-skinned characters are usually either sidekicks to the White hero or they are the bad guys. The White cop captures the Black criminal; the blond-hair teacher tutors an underprivileged Black student after school while the Black custodian sweeps the classroom floors in the background; the rapper belts out his lyrics while barely-clothed Black girls grind on the rapper's legs. Children's shows aren't exempt. Take, for example, any popular "princess" movie. Overwhelmingly, the starring princesses are White (or very light skinned) and they have long, straight hair (not typical of many minority children). These characters also tend to have European-looking features, even when they are supposedly of another race (American Indian, in the case of Pocahontas, or Asian, in the case of Mulan). Princess Tiana's hair is long and flowing, not kinky or curly or in an afro-style. (Since the movie is made for young children, many of whom have not yet reached the age where having their hair straightened is a self-selected option, it seems that the first Black princess should have hair representative of that of the young, Black community.) The message that "brown is bad" or isn't-as-good-as-white-and-thus-must-be-changed, is consistently being sent to children and adults.

Children need to see that people of their own race can be successful adults. There is nothing wrong with someone being a janitor or a cook or a roofer, for example, but depending on where you live, your child might see people of his or her race in these positions but not in a position of higher pay and status, such as a doctor, lawyer, store owner, or school principal.

If you live in a place where Black adults are not consistently seen in prestigious positions and you do not currently have the option of moving to another community, don't give up. Refer back to the list of environments to evaluate. Where can you meet people whom you might befriend and who might, in the future, serve as a real-life racial role model for your child?

The point is, parents need to create opportunities to better their success as transracial adoptive parents. Parenting is work for any parent, but for transracial adoptive parents, there are more challenging tasks, including genuinely and purposefully embracing people who share their child's race.

The media will be your child's most prominent racial teacher if you choose not to be. With all the negative messages the media sends about people of color, consciously and subconsciously, it's clearly evident that adoptive parents have to take deliberate steps to combat them.

Questions from the Trenches

I want to approach people of my child's race, but I feel incredibly awkward. I just can't bring myself to take that first step and introduce myself. What can I do?

First, ask yourself why you feel awkward. Are you a naturally shy person? Are you afraid of being judged? Are you ashamed to be "targeting" someone of your child's race? Have you fully addressed the loss that led you to adopt? Has a negative past experience been hindering you?

Second, consider seeking help overcoming particularly oppressive issues that not only hinder your ability to approach new people but might also hamper you in effectively parenting your child.

When approaching someone new, know that there is one favorite subject for most people: themselves. Topics you might ask about include where the person works, his or her hobbies, his or her family. If you notice that the person's child has a nice haircut, ask the parent for the name of the child's barber shop or stylist.

Approaching anyone can be intimidating, but practice makes perfect. If you begin to see people as potential friends instead of judges, you will create possibilities and demonstrate to your child that making new friends, despite racial differences, can be rewarding.

My child is not only transracially adopted, but she also has some physical disabilities that make her stand out even more. I'm afraid that we won't fit in with most adoption support groups. I think my family is an anomaly among an already small and defined group.

Something that all adoptive parents seem to grasp is the concept of difference and the positive and negative impacts it can have on the entire family. You may not find another child exactly like yours in a support group, but you will likely find understanding and supportive members.

One benefit to being part of a support group is that adoptive parents seem to be aware of the best resources. Adoptive parents I know have connections that even agency workers and attorneys do not. By joining a support group, you might learn of other groups and resources that you weren't previously aware of.

You need to offer support groups the same opportunity you want for your daughter: the opportunity to be welcomed without judgment. You never know what connections you will make among other adoptive families.

My child's teacher assigned each child a historical figure on whom he or she must write a report. I'm a bit disheartened that my son was assigned a White historical figure. I was hoping he would be assigned to learn more about someone of his own race. Should I say anything to the teacher or let it be?

Instead of demanding that the teacher allow your child to report on a Black historical figure, find out more about the assignment. Were any Black historical figures assigned? What is the purpose of the assignment? Why weren't the children allowed to choose their own figures? It is likely that the teacher has thoroughly planned the purpose, execution, and desired outcome of the assignment, though it's also perfectly reasonable for you, as the parent, to ask questions.

Ask your child how he feels about the assignment without purposefully leading your child to the conclusion you desire. Perhaps your child is excited about being assigned Abraham Lincoln. If so, should your preferences trump your child's? If your child has an interest in another historical figure, whether that person is Black or of another race, should you encourage or help your child to talk to the teacher?

As with many homework assignments, you will likely be helping your child to navigate and fulfill the assignment. One option is to look for some link between the historical figure and the Black community; your child might choose to share that within the report. However, the transracially adopted child shouldn't be burdened with turning every assignment into a lesson on race or adoption or both.

Transracial adoptive parents walk a fine line between encouraging their children to develop a healthy racial identity while not over-emphasizing race. As parents, we have the task of guiding and overseeing our children and their well-being, but we must balance this with our children's desires and needs.

Despite the fact that we live in a racially diverse area and my teenage son attends a diverse school, the vast majority of his friends are White. He is nearing dating-age, and all of the girls he's been interested in are White. I'm concerned that I've failed him in some way. Should I encourage him to befriend and date kids of his race?

When I enrolled my oldest in her first year of preschool, I was thrilled that there was another brown-skinned girl in her class. I would occasionally ask my daughter if she played with this little girl, to which my daughter always said no. One day I asked my child's teachers who my daughter played with. The response was interesting: she played with two little boys, frequently at the train table. It dawned on me that my daughter, though she pointed out kids whose skin color matched hers, formed friendships based on interests, not on race, gender, age, or ability. What she cared about most was simply playing with toy trains. She wanted to share that experience with those who had the same interest.

As parents, we focus on making sure our children have opportunities to interact with people of many races, but particularly people of our child's own race. Yet, as our children get older and are no longer under our complete control, their preferences begin to emerge, and they might not be what we expected, planned, or hoped for.

My husband and I often joke that right now, the majority or our extended family is White, but we will become the minority in our immediate family as it grows, since our current children are Black and our future children will likely be Black or multiracial. We picture a time when we are older and get together with our kids and their families. Will we be the only White people in attendance? Maybe. But then again, maybe not. What adoption has taught us is that there are many possibilities in life, and we have to be willing to embrace the unexpected in order to receive the blessings that come with it.

So to answer your question, my fellow well-seasoned adoptive parents have told me that their transracially adopted kids have a variety of preferences when it comes to forming friendships and dating. If you see a red-flag issue, you should, of course, address it. Otherwise, go with the flow.

Questions for Further Discussion

- What aspects of adoption do I find most isolating?

- Have I joined an adoptive parent support group? Why or why not? Is my group a good fit for me and my family?

- How many transracial adoptive families have I befriended? What can I do to increase my contact with them?

- Who is my adoption mentor? If I don't have one right now, who might be a good candidate?

- Do I know any new adoptive parents or prospective adoptive parents whom I could offer to mentor?

- What are one or two specific ways I can create more opportunities for diversity in my family's life?

- How many true friends do I have who racially match my child? (If you can name acquaintances but not friends, make it a point to communicate more to see if a friendship is possible.)

Practical Application

If you are a new adoptive parent, write a letter of gratitude to someone who helped (or is helping) you or is helping you to navigate the adoption and parenting journey. List specific ways the person supported and encouraged you.

If you are a seasoned adoptive parent, make it a point to reach out to a prospective or new adoptive parent in the coming week. Offer to help in the ways others helped you when you were new to adoption.

Resources for Parents:

Effective Support Groups (James E. Miller)

How To Win Friends and Influence People (Dale Carnegie)

Making Small Groups Work: What Every Small Group Leader Needs to Know (Henry Cloud and John Townsend)

The Support Group Manual: A Session-By-Session Guide (Harriet Sarnoff Schiff)

http://adoptivefamilies.com/support_group.php
Meetup.com

Resources for Kids:

All the World (Liza Garton Scanlon)

Amazing Faces (Lee Bennett Hopkins)

A Rainbow of Friends (P.K. Hallinan)

Each Kindness (Jacqueline Woodson)

Happy to Be Nappy and Other Stories of Me (DVD)

How To Make an Apple Pie and See the World (Marjorie Priceman)

I Have the Right to Be a Child (Alain Serres)

It's a Small World (Richard M. Sherman and Robert B. Sherman)

Little Sweet Potato (Amy Beth Bloom)

Ones and Twos (Marthe Jocelyn and Nell Jocelyn)

Orange Peel's Pocket (Rose A. Lewis)

Sidewalk Chalk: Poems of the City (Carole Boston Weatherford)

Think Big (Liz Garton Scanlon)

Whole World (Christopher Corr and Fred Penner)

CHAPTER NINE

"I Was In Her Belly Button": Discussing Adoption and Race With Children

"No matter how much she loves her family, no matter how secure she is in her adoption, it's important to recognize that the child has first experienced loss in order to become part of her family."

~ELISABETH O'TOOLE, IN ON IT: WHAT ADOPTIVE PARENTS WOULD LIKE YOU TO KNOW ABOUT ADOPTION

"Adoptees, like any other group of people, occupy the full spectrum of personality types and individual circumstances."

~ADAM PERTMAN, ADOPTION NATION: HOW THE ADOPTION REVOLUTION IS TRANSFORMING OUR FAMILIES — AND AMERICA

When my daughter was two years old, I had yet another adoption conversation with her. She had recently started recognizing her birth mother in photographs, joyfully pointing to her face and saying her first name. I said to her, "Yes, that is your birth mother." My two-year-old surprised and delighted me with her response: "I was in her belly button."

A year later, my daughter was walking around our home "talking" on one of our old cell phones. She handed me the phone and said that it was her birth mother and she wanted to speak with me. My daughter continued by saying that her birth mother wanted me to go in a space-ship with her. I took the call and continued the "conversation" while my daughter stood nearby, grinning.

These moments in my daughter's life make me smile. It's clearly evident that the repetition of my daughter's adoption story resonates with her.

You see, when you adopt transracially, there's no concealing the adoption. Wherever you go, whomever you are surrounded by, adoption will inevitably come up—whether in a comment, a question, or even a look.

Unlike my White friends who have adopted White children, I don't always get to decide when adoption discussions will occur. For example, my husband took our youngest daughter to the grocery store with him one evening. As he was placing fruit in his cart, two women asked him if the child was his daughter. He said yes, and they asked if she was adopted. He replied that yes, she was, and the ladies then asked if she had been adopted from foster care. My husband said no, and the ladies walked away, seconds later running their cart into a display. We found the mishap quite humorous: Just like a store display, adoption and race conversations can take your family by surprise.

This chapter is designed to further your understanding of many adoption and race topics, to empower you to talk to your child about adoption and race, and to encourage you to make adoption and race a continual conversation in your home—one that is welcomed.

Struggling to Speak

Adoption isn't a topic that parents inherently know how to talk about due to adoption's complexity, the parent's feelings about adoption and past losses, and the circumstances surrounding the child's placement. Some adoptions entail adoptive parents facing some harsh past and present realities: drug or alcohol abuse, rape, neglect, abuse, psychological disorders, abortion, and more. Naturally, parents want to shield their children from confusion, rejection, anger, and sadness. However, if adoptive parents are to be trusted by their children, they must be transparent about the truth.

The authors of *The Whole Life Adoption Book: Realistic Advice for Building A Healthy Adoptive Family* outline why some adoptive parents "struggle with talking about adoption" (182). They say such things as:

- "I fear my child might feel a lesser part of the family."

- "I fear I will lose his love."

- "It isn't the right time."

- "It will devastate her self-esteem."

- "I don't feel I have the skill."

However, I believe that when an adoptive parent is armed with resources, he or she is perfectly capable to discuss adoption with the child in a productive way. This isn't to say that adoption-talk will produce what the parent deems to be a perfect, much-desired response (positive, clean, and accepting). Keep in mind, you will not always have the answers to your child's inquiries. Embrace the fact that you don't know it all, and when you don't have an answer, speak that fact to your child.

Remember, you were selected by a social worker, agency, or birth parent to be your child's parent. Being a parent comes with responsibilities that are often undesirable and uncomfortable. However, just because you are personally struggling does not mean that you have permission to inflict struggles upon your child.

Adam Pertman writes in *Adoption Nation: How the Adoption Revolution is Transforming Our Families — and America*: "The more secure adoptive parents grow, the more concretely they internalize the understanding that their children aren't confused about who their 'real' parents are: the people who hug them, help them with their homework, tuck them into bed. And the more confident adoptive parents become, the less intimidated they are by the notion that their kids might also be able to love other people, like grandfathers or aunts or birth parents, without its posing a threat to their own relationships" (177).

The Primal Wound

Nancy Newton Verrier, author of the controversial book *The Primal Wound: Understanding the Adopted Child*, states, "Many doctors and psychologists now understand that bonding doesn't begin at birth, but is a continuum of physiological, psychological, and spiritual events which begin in utero and continue throughout the postnatal bonding period. When this natural evolution is interrupted by a postnatal separation from the biological mother, the resultant experience of abandonment and loss is indelibly imprinted upon the unconscious minds of these children, causing that which I call the 'primal wound'" (1). All adopted children, whether they were separated from one parent (the birth parent) or multiple parents (nannies, foster parents, birth relatives), come to their adoptive family with the primal wound.

I was quite resistant to this idea early in my adoption education. I wanted to believe that I was enough parent for my child, that indeed he or she wouldn't have an "imprint" or a "wound." The whole concept of the primal wound not only hurt my pride as a mother, but it also made me feel as though my children would all be or become emotionally or psychologically disabled simply because they were adopted.

Instead of continuing to resist the concept of the primal wound, I have learned to engage with and embrace it, accepting that it is a part of every adopted child's life and might very well surface and resurface as the adoptee grows up. For example, when Verrier discusses birthdays in her book, she says, "Many clinicians and parents have told me that adoptees often act out a great deal before and during their birthday parties. They begin by having a sense of excitement, but often end up sabotaging the whole affair. [...] Why would one want to celebrate the day they were separated from their mothers? The adoptees, of course, have probably never really understood, themselves, why they do this" (16). She continues to say that an adopted child's birthday "commemorate[s] an experience, not of joy, but one of loss and sorrow" (16).

Adoptive parents often begin their understanding of a child at the age the child comes home: infant, toddler, preschooler, elementary-age child, pre-teen, or teen. Why? Because this is when our journey with the child begins. But we must remember that there was a time, in-utero, when the child and his or her biological mother were "psychologically one" (17). As the baby transitions "from the warm, fluid, dark security of the womb to the cold, bright, alien world of postnatal life" the "baby needs to be in proximity to his mother in order to find the world safe and welcoming instead of confusing, uncaring, and hostile. At that time the mother is the whole world for the baby, and his connection to her is essential to his sense of well-being and wholeness" (21). This break in oneness creates the "primal wound."

I encourage you to read Verrier's book to gain further understanding of the concept, including how it relates to loss, healing, identity, trust, intimacy, and rejection. Though these ideas make adoptive parents uncomfortable, Verrier offers hope and empowerment. She concludes, "Adoptive parents need to be assured that adopting a child is very important, and that they need not consider themselves failures as parents if their children seem unable to respond as they or others expect. The life of the family has begun with a handicap—their child's short, but profound, immediate post-natal-history—a span of time which has largely been ignored by parents and professionals as having anything to do with what is going on in adoptive family life. Yet, in my opinion, *it is quintessential to understanding the dynamics of the adoptive family*" (219).

Loss and the Adopted Child

Beyond the "primal wound," adopted children face additional losses, as outlined by Elizabeth O'Toole in her book *In On It: What Adoptive Parents Would Like You To Know About Adoption*. These include the loss of "a genetic connection," "knowledge of birth culture" ("possibly including language, customs, history, religion, citizenship"), "knowledge of biological relatives and family history," "of other relationships (foster parents, caregivers, friends, etc.)," "control (children don't 'choose' to be adopted [...])," "a sense of normalcy, of being 'like everybody else,'" and "of confidence in the stability and security of their family (i.e., fear of future abandonment)" (45).

Adoptive parents need to be aware of these losses and understand that they may creep up simultaneously or individually throughout the child's life. Some children may not voluntarily voice their feelings, some may not be old enough to articulate losses, and some may not even be aware that a certain behavior is reaction to loss. Parents who create and maintain an open door to adoption-related discussions demonstrate to their children that it's OK to talk about loss and to express emotions related to adoption loss.

Nature vs. Nurture

How much of a child's personality, preferences, and quirks come from his or her biological parents? How much comes from the child's past caregivers? How much comes from the adoptive parents?

Adoption experts seem to agree that it's important for a child's sense of belonging within the adoptive family that both nature and nurture are embraced. Adopted children are a wonderful mix of their birth families, their adoptive families, their environments, and their birth order. Mary Watkins and Susan Fisher share in *Talking With Young Children About Adoption*, "Almost no one today would argue that fundamental personal qualities such as intelligence, interest, abilities, and character are either strictly biological or strictly environmental. There is a broad consensus that nature and nurture are interactive, that the presenting characteristics of the child and the environment in which he lives affect each other" (49).

Elisabeth O'Toole shares in her book *In On It: What Adoptive Parents Would Like You To Know About Adoption* that "it's important to recognize that adoption doesn't have to mean forgoing family resemblances. A child raised in a family of readers is likely to share an appreciation for literature. If Grandma plays piano, it's going to go down in the family history that the child played piano 'just like Grandma did.' As a prospective adoptive parent, I recall feeling gratified as I listened to an adoptive father and his son describe how they shared an identical goofy sense of humor" (36).

I recall my younger sister calling to say that she had just stumbled upon a photo of me as a toddler. She said I was standing in a particular way (it was probably quite sassy and self-assured as many oldest children are) that reminded her exactly of my oldest daughter. I remember laughing and thinking, *How could that be? My daughter and I have no genetic ties.*

The older my children get, the more I see both their birth families and us, their adoptive parents, in them. My oldest daughter laughs just like her biological brother and gets easily frustrated just like me. My younger daughter is a spitting image of her birth father and loves to get into mischief just as my younger sister did when she was little.

Learning About and Understanding Adoption and Race: An Age-by-Age Guide

In this section, you will learn about what your child might understand and need to know, age by age, on the subjects of adoption and race. Adoption and race, though very different topics, sometimes intersect in transracial adoption. Children who are transracially adopted will have adoption brought to their attention more often than a child who is adopted by a family of his or her own race, because the adoption is so obvious. Thus, it's important that adoption and race not be treated as isolated from one another in discussions.

Infants and Toddlers

Adoption experts agree that your child is never too young to hear his or her adoption story; children this young can be told simplified versions. At this point in a child's life, sharing the story with him or her mainly benefits the adoptive parent: it is an opportunity for practice. However, by toddlerhood, your child quickly learns the words you repeat often ("adoption," "birth parent," the child's place of birth, etc.), even before learning their meanings. Adoption talk at this age might include reading a simple book, praying for the child's biological family members aloud, or pointing at photos of birth-family members, previous caregivers, or photos taken from the child's home country and using simple words to refer to their people and places. You may also have a special object, such as a blanket, that has adoption-journey significance.

Lois Ruskai Melina and Sharon Kaplan Roszia, authors of *The Open Adoption Experience*, warn adoptive parents to avoid telling the child that he or she is "special" because of the adoption. They recommend, instead, that you "show him how special he is to you" to avoid the child feeling as if he must "remain special to stay in his adoptive family" (249). Furthermore, "Rather than telling him he was placed because his birth parents loved him so much, the birth parents can just demonstrate their affection and concern for him" (249). If you do not have an open adoption with your child's birth family or you rarely see or speak with them, you can supplement. We do have open adoptions, but visits occur only a few times a year. Therefore, I do step in for the birth parents and tell my children that their birth parents love them very much, which I know is true.

Though children this young do not understand race, they can see color. Take, for example, the groundbreaking *Newsweek* article entitled "See Baby Discriminate," which asks: "How do researchers test a 6-month-old [for racial awareness]? They show babies photographs of faces. Katz found that babies will stare significantly longer at photographs of faces that are a different race from their parents, indicating they find the face out of the ordinary. Race itself has no ethnic meaning per se—but children's brains are noticing skin-color differences and trying to understand their meaning." When my oldest child was young, she would often spend significant lengths of time staring at my friend who is Guatemalan. My friend's caramel skin was of interest to my daughter and was contrasted by my "pink" skin.

Preschoolers and Young School Age Children

Preschoolers and young children are incredibly interesting. Not only are they quite literal in their thinking and speaking, but they never seem to stop talking. Their imaginations run wild. Betsy Keefer and Jayne E. Schooler, authors of *Telling the Truth to Your Adopted or Foster Child* state that adoptive parents should *"encourage questions and answer concretely and simply"* (57). Further suggestions include correcting the child when he or she plays out his or her adoption inaccurately, tell the child his or her adoption story often, and remind the child that the adoptive family is the child's forever family (57-58). (A favorite line in our household is: "Families are forever!") Keep in mind, as Patricia Irwin Johnston shares in *Adoption is a Family Affair*, "At pre-school or kindergarten most adopted children are first exposed to others' negative bias about adoption" (107). As children get a little older, they will begin to feel "responsible for everything that happens around them" including their adoptions, and many will wonder why they were adopted (108). Johnston warns adoptive parents that some children will not be openly vocal about their feelings; Keefer and Schooler advise adoptive parents to encourage their child to ask questions and express feelings. Melina and Roszia note that though children can often repeat and understand parts of their adoption stories, the concept of adoption is still quite abstract, and will continue to be until "they can understand reproduction" (249).

Preschoolers are often interested in matching and begin to discover the differences between themselves and others—gender and race included. Many parents dread this age as children might point out that the other person in the checkout line is overweight or that someone is in a wheelchair. My oldest daughter, at age three, was greatly intrigued by other brown-skinned children and women with afros, and she would, without reservation, loudly and clearly point out that someone nearby was "brown" like her or had a "big crazy afro." It's important to note that though many White adults embrace the idea that "race doesn't matter" and that "racism is a thing of the past," neither of these is true. Any experienced transracial adoptive family can testify that race does matter and that the world is not colorblind. As Beverly Daniel Tatum explains in *"Why Are All the Black Kids Sitting Together in the Cafeteria?": And Other Conversations About Race,* "Many adults do not know how to respond when children make race-related observations" and "children who have been silenced often enough learn not to talk about race publicly. Their questions don't go away, they just go unasked" (36).

Very young children also internalize stereotypes, as explained by Tatum. She writes that one of her students "conducted a research project investigating preschoolers' concepts of Native Americans," asking the three-and four-year-old participants to "draw a picture of a Native American" (4). The children were baffled by the request, so the researcher re-phrased, asking the children to "draw a picture of an Indian" (4). The researcher found that "Almost every picture included one central feature: feathers. In fact, many of them also included a weapon—a knife or tomahawk—and depicted the person in violent or aggressive terms" (4). Tatum notes that most of the students were White and "did not live near a large Native American population and probably had had little if any personal interaction with American Indians" yet they were able to produce a drawing of an Indian. The researcher found that the children referenced Disney's *Peter Pan* as their "number-one source of information" (4). This is just one example, but it demonstrates that the media is a powerful influence on young children. Parents should carefully select what movies, television shows, and books are and are not appropriate.

Mid-School Age to Pre-Teen

Keefer and Schooler state that around age seven or eight, "children understand the concept of adoption for the first time" because they are able to understand sex and conception (58). Parents need to initiate the "birds and the bees" discussion with their child. Keefer and Schooler advise adoptive parents to continue to initiate adoption conversations with children and to be aware that children many have "anniversary reactions" (such as, the authors point out, on the child's adoption day or birthday). "Let children know they can love two sets of parents" (59-60). Melina and Roszia state that a child from ages seven to eleven will "become more interested in the father's role in reproduction" and "may want a lot more information about his birth father" (252-253). Children this age might also become more interested in any biological siblings and want to know why they were placed for adoption (253). This is also a time in a child's life when feelings of insecurity, embarrassment, and grief begin to emerge, according to the authors, and children this age have "active imaginations" that can create fantasies about birth families (255-261). Last, the child is nearing puberty, so his or her body is beginning to change and the child's "abilities, interests, and talents become more developed," both of which can show the child's "similarity to the birth parents" (262).

Parents should continue to be open and honest about transracial adoption. Asking the child open-ended questions is preferable to asking questions that can be answered with a simple yes, no, or grunt responses typical of many children this age. Children may be more or less likely to respond to the race and adoption questions of strangers, family members, and peers, depending on the child's emotional state at the time. Parents should have frequent conversations with their children, asking how situations should be handled and who will handle them.

Teenagers

Children at this age are constantly striving for independence and identity. As the authors of *Being Adopted: The Lifelong Search for Self* state, "Peer relationships become extremely important" and teens have a "desperate need to conform" which can "present special problems for the adopted teenager, who may feel different from other people because she doesn't know much about her past" and perhaps lives "in a community where few other youngsters are adopted" (96). Hormonal changes during this time can increase tension between parents and the child, and adoption can exacerbate struggles. Keefer and Schooler suggest that adoptive parents avoid *"responding to the child's anger with more anger"* and let the child exercise control within reason, but also to remain the parent (62-63). Johnston states that many children this age begin seriously contemplating a search for more information about their adoption and even a search for biological family members (109). Some teenagers also worry that they will '"repeat their birthparents' mistakes'" (109). A teen's greater interest in sex and sexuality leads many adoptive parents into more frequent discussions about their child's adoption story, contraception, and the implications of being sexually active.

In Being Adopted: The Lifelong Search for Self, the authors share, "As they spend hours primping and fretting before the mirror, adolescents tend to rely on physical markings as keys to their identity" and the physical (and often rapid) changes teens see "can be disorienting" (97). The teen may "spend more and more time thinking about her looks" and "be troubled by the fact that she doesn't seem to fit in physically with the rest of the family" (97). The transracially adopted child has likely been aware for quite some time, that he or she is physically quite different from the adoptive parents, but with yearning to conform might well bring emphasis on differences. The authors note that "Not only are transracial adoptees physically different, they are culturally different, too. And because adolescence is the period when cultural, ethnic, or racial identity comes to the fore, the conflict between the child's ethnicity and the familyies can be another source of trouble. Issues of identity can get confused for young-sters who look one way and are raised another" (99).

Beverly Daniel Tatum writes in *"Why Are All The Black Kids Sitting Together in the Cafeteria?": And Other Conversations About Race,* "Why do Black youths, in particular, think about themselves in terms of race? Because that is how the rest of the world thinks of them. Our self-perceptions are shaped by the messages that we receive from those around us, and when young Black men and women enter adolescence, the racial con-tent of those messages intensifies" (54). As many transracial adoptees testified in *In Their Own Voices: Transracial Adoptees Tell Their Stories,* children who previously seemed content to be part of a transracial family might find themselves strug-gling during their teenage years, particularly when adoptive parents have neglected to provide children with racial support such as access to meaningful relationships with people of the child's own race.

Who? What? When? Where? Why? How?

Talking about adoption, especially the not-so-pretty parts, can be incredibly difficult for adoptive parents. Naturally, parents want to shield their children from any ugly truths that could lead to their children feeling ashamed, sad, confused, or angry.

The authors of *Telling the Truth to Your Adopted or Foster Child* share their "Ten Commandments of Telling" (87-96). I will list the commandments here, but I encourage you to read their book in the near-future to gain further insight. The authors offer real-life examples, analogies, and further instruction with each Commandment. These adoption commandments can double as rules for racial discussions as well.

1: Initiate Conversation About Adoption.
2: Use Positive Adoption Language
3: Never Lie to a Child About the Past or a Birth Family Member.

4: Allow a Child to Express Anger Toward a Birth Family Member Without Joining In.

5: Omissions Are Okay Until Age Twelve. After That, all Information Should Be Shared.

6: If Information is Negative, Use a Third Party, Such as a Therapist, to Relate the Most Troublesome Details.

7: Don't Try to "Fix" the Pain of Adoption.

8: Don't Impose Value Judgments on the Information.

9: A Child Should Have Control of Telling His or Her Story Outside the Immediate Family.

10: Remember That the Child Probably Knows More Than You Think He or She Does.

Adoption books often remark how important it is to listen to our children — to "acknowledge the authenticity of our children's feelings (and be grateful when they express them)" (Alperson 168).

Incorporating and Explaining Adoption in Everyday Life

There are several ways adoptive parents can explore and explain adoption to their children. Depending on how your child came to you, the child's history, the amount of information you have, and the level of openness you have with the child's birth family, you can determine which of these suggestions best suits your family.

I am not suggesting that adoptive parents continuously (or randomly) throw adoption conversations at the child "out of left field." However, many adoptive parents tell me that their children simply do not care about adoption when, in fact, the parents have chosen not to ask the child how he or she feels about adoption or if there's anything the child feels that he or she needs to discuss with the parent or with a professional. The key is to keep communication open, because when a child is transracially adopted, adoption and race issues will inevitably arise throughout the child's life. Don't leave it up to your child to bring up such issues. You are the parent.

One of the most common tools adoptive parents use to explain adoption is a lifebook. A lifebook is a book adoptive parents create for their child that tells the child adoption story. It might include mementos like ticket stubs, special papers (birth certificate, a letter from a previous caregiver or birth parent, etc.), and photographs. There are many benefits to creating a lifebook, according to Arleta James, author of *Brothers and Sisters in Adoption* (362):

- "It helps the adoptee make sense of her experience."

- "It separates fact from fantasy."

- "It enhances attachment. The child physiologically separates from previous caregivers."

- "It brings about behavior changes" by changing "irrational thinking."

- "It facilitates grief for the loss of birthfamily, siblings, foster families, familiar surroundings and items, and traumatic experiences."

- "It identifies positive and negatives about the birthfamily."

Other options include:

- *Take a trip.* When possible, see the hospital where your child was born, visit the child's former caregiver or social worker, explore your child's birth town. If your child was born in another country, this can be more of a challenge, so get creative. View videos or read books and magazines with your child about his or her birth country. Display a world map in your home where you can point out where you live now and where the child was born. Invite someone who lived in your child's birth country to have dinner with your family and talk about the birth country's culture and traditions. One trip may not be enough for a child, but international travel can be costly and time-consuming, so adoptive families should negotiate how many trips can be taken and at what stages in their child's lives these trips are the most healthy and appropriate.

- *Build an adoption library.* An in-home adoption library of books and videos benefit both the parent and child as an on-hand resource for addressing adoption questions as they arise. Adoption discussions are often impromptu, whether prompted by the child or the parent. Many of the resources I list in this book are for children. I suggest previewing resources for appropriateness: borrow books and videos from the library before purchasing. Don't forget you can also buy them used.

- *Use photographs.* Display photos of your child's birth family as appropriate, if you have them, so that your child can see the person's face, become accustomed to his or her name, and know that you, as the parent, are comfortable talking about adoption. Photos can be placed in a child's room, in a more public area like a living room, or in a photo album that the child can take out or put away as he or she wishes.

- *Create a life map.* Keefer and Schooler explain that a life map can be helpful for children adopted from foster care or children adopted internationally. Included on this hand-drawn map might be: "where the child has lived," "how long he lived there," "the people, pets, places that were important to him," "why he had to move," and "how he felt about the move" (120).

- *Use art and play therapy.* You may not be a therapist, but you can use art and play therapy's principles to explore adoption with your child. Options include playing out an adoption situation with dolls or action figures or drawing a picture based on an adoption-related feeling or situation.

Questions from the Trenches

At a family gathering, one of my second cousins asked, in front of the entire family, what my newly adopted daughter's "story" was. I blurted out some information, and now I regret it. How can I respond better the next time I'm asked an untimely and inappropriate question?

It's likely that your family member felt as if he or she was owed this information, being that the child is now a part of the family. And, concurrently, the family member likely didn't realize that asking for intimate details about your child's adoption is inappropriate and can be harmful to the child.

One way to respond is to give general, non-invasive information. You might say when your child was born, the general area where your child is from, and how excited you were to be matched or referred to your child. You then might demonstrate that the conversation is over by saying, "Thanks for asking!" and then turn your attention elsewhere.

Another response, one that many adoptive parents shy away from for fear of being perceived as secretive or ashamed, is to simply say, "Thanks for asking about my daughter. I'm so happy to be a new dad" (evasive), or, "My child's adoption story belongs to her, so we have decided to let her share as much or as little of her story as she chooses" (giving power to the child), or, "That's information we don't share outside of our immediate family." Remember, your role is to provide and protect your child, and you must set aside your feelings or perceived obligations to your family for the sake of your child.

Revisit your family's disclosure plan often and make revisions when necessary. If your child is old enough, you should incorporate your child into disclosure decisions. However, as the adult, you understand the implications of any decisions you and your child make, so allow the child to contribute within reason.

My preschooler has made some comments recently that have me concerned. One day she said she wanted to have light skin, like me. How can I respond?

Tatum states in her book, "The concept of race constancy, that one's racial group membership is fixed and will not change, is not achieved until children are six or seven years old. (The same is true of gender constancy.) Just as preschool boys sometimes express a desire to have a baby like Mom when they grow up (and are dismayed when they learn they cannot), young Black children may express a desire to be White. Though such statements are certainly distressing to parents, they do not necessarily mean that the child has internalized a negative self-image. It may, however, reflect a child's growing awareness of White privilege, conveyed through the media" (43).

It's difficult to know where a skin-color thought comes from. It could be the media, a question or comment made by someone in your child's class, or something else. Tatum states, "Though such comments by young children are not necessarily rooted in self-rejection, it is important to consider what messages children are receiving about the relative worth of light or dark skin" (43). Parents, as much as possible, should monitor who and what their children are being exposed to.

Practically, a fellow adoptive mom to a brown-skinned four-year-old suggests that parents respond to a preschoolers skin-color comment with a compliment. Something like, "I love your skin. It's beautiful brown!" Adoptive parents might also choose to read books to their children, books listed in chapter 5, which focus on the beauty of the range of skin, eye, and hair colors.

My young teenage son got very upset with me the other day and said he wanted to go live with his birth parents. I was heartbroken when he said this. How should I respond?

This situation can be looked at in a few ways. First, the "I'm going to go live with my birth father!" could simply be a version of a biological child yelling, "I hate you!" to his or her biological parent. We all have said things we do not mean in the heat of the moment.

Secondly, it could demonstrate that your child doesn't have an accurate view of what life with his or her birth parent might entail. It's common for adoptees to have fantasies about birth parents and what life with them might look like. This is especially true of the child has little to no information about his or her birth parents or has an inaccurate understanding of the situation because either you have chosen not to share harsh truths or because any communication, such as visits, occurs in a neutral environment where the birth parent's living situation isn't visible. Another possibility is that the child has communication with a biological parent, sibling, or other relative who paints a "perfect picture" of their lives, be it reality or not.

Thirdly, your child could be expressing his or her need to discuss adoption. Evaluate how often and to what degree you talk about adoption in your home. Communicating with a teenager can be incredibly trying, but that doesn't mean you should cease to initiate and engage in adoption conversations with your child. Particularly, a transracially adopted child is obviously different from his or her family and this contradicts teenage culture which values sameness and standards.

If you find that this type of comment persists, seeking professional help could be helpful. However, if the comment happened only once, you might have to swallow your pride (and hurt feelings) and move forward, knowing that you have to choose your battles. However, you must also draw the line at what type of frustration (verbal outbursts, physical aggression such as door-slamming, etc.) is and isn't appropriate in your home.

My child was assigned a project involving family history. I'm unsure how I should direct my child in the assignment, being that we aren't genetically related to her. Should I ask the teacher for an alternative assignment?

This assignment could offer you, as the parent, a great opportunity to have an open and honest adoption and race conversation with your child. Before you demand that your child's teacher offer an alternative assignment, which could convey to your child that you are somehow embarrassed or uncomfortable with adoption and race, consider the other options.

There are a number of ways you can respond to this situation, but the first place to start is to ask the child, the one whose name will be on the assignment and the one who will be graded on her work, what she would like to do. As a college teacher, I can tell you that students need to understand that they should take ownership in their work and turn in a product they are proud of. See if your child suggests what she'd like to do and additionally, offer some other options.

Other options might include expanding the assignment to fit the family's unique makeup. If your child was assigned a family tree, you might, instead, suggest a family orchard. Some students may choose to draw a family tree with roots in which the roots represent birth family members. If the assignment involves genetics, the child can choose to share birth family information, if the information is available and the child is comfortable sharing this information, or the student might ask the teacher what alternatives there are to the original assignment. If photographs are involved in the project, students can choose to draw a representation of a birth family member or use photographs of the adoptive family. Adoptive parents can discuss with children the consequences, both positive and negative, that might result from choosing to do the assignment in a particular way. Parents might also have a frank discussion with the teacher or administration about offering alternatives from the get-go or altering the assignment completely, given that not all members of any given family are biologically related.

Assessing your child's age, maturity level, and life stage will help you guide the child when it comes to potentially sticky assignments. Ultimately, support your child, even if he or she chooses to do the assignment in a way you don't prefer. The key is to show your child, with your actions and reactions, that you accept and love the child and respect his or her decisions when it comes to the child's life story and racial makeup.

Questions for Further Discussion

- What fears and struggles do you face when it comes to talking to your child about adoption? What steps can you take to relieve these fears and resolve struggles?

- What questions and concerns do you have about the primal wound? Is this a concept you have heard about prior to reading this book?

- What losses regarding adoption is your child currently struggling with most? If no losses are evident, have you spoken about adoption and loss recently with your child?

- What characteristics does your child possess that are similar to that of an adoptive family member? What characteristics remind you of the child's birth family?

- Review "The Ten Commandments of Telling." Which do you struggle with most? Why?

- What steps can you take to embrace and incorporate adoption more into your family's everyday life?

Practical Application

Watch an adoption-themed film with your family and discuss how adoption was handled in the film. How does this film relate to your own family's adoption journey? (Parents should view the films beforehand to determine their appropriateness). Suggested films include: *The Odd Life of Timothy Green, Kung Fu Panda 2,*

Annie, Pollyanna, Elf, Anne of Green Gables, The Little Princess, Prince of Egypt, Tarzan, A Smoky Mountain Christmas, Tangled, Curious George, Corduroy, Hotel for Dogs, A Mama for Owen, Despicable Me, Stuart Little, Meet the Robinsons. Older children might be interested to watch *The Blind Side, White Oleander, Like Dandelion Dust, August Rush, My Own Love Song, Losing Isaiah, Raising Helen, Antwone Fisher.*

Using a large cardboard box, trace and cut out a tree with one main branch per adopted child. At the base of the tree, put a photo of your family. At the base of each branch, put a photo of the child. Higher up the branch, place a photo of the child's biological parents. (If you do not have photos of birth family members, have your child draw a representation or cut out representations from magazines). On branches connected to the main branch, place photos of birth siblings and other birth family members. Use this family tree to explain and explore adoption with your child.

Resources for Adoptive Parents

A Child Called It (Dave Pelzer)

Before You Were Mine: Discovering Your Adopted Child's Lifestory (Sara TeBos and Carissa Woodwyk)

Being Lara (Lola Jayne)

I Beat the Odds: From Homelessness to The Blind Side (Michael Oher and Don Yeager)

I'm Chocolate, You're Vanilla: Raising Healthy Black and Biracial Children in a Race-Conscious World (Marguerite A. Wright)

Lifebooks: Creating a Treasure for the Adopted Child (Beth O'Malley)

Nurture the Nature: Understanding and Supporting Your Child's Unique Core Personality (Michael Gurian)

Oranges and Sunshine (DVD)

Raising Adopted Children (Lois Ruskai Melina)

Real Parents, Real Children: Parenting the Adopted Child (Holly van Gulden and Lisa M. Bartels-Rabb)

Searching For a Past: The Adopted Adult's Unique Process of Finding Identity (Jayne Schooler)

Telling the Truth to Your Adopted or Foster Child (Betsy Keefer and Jayne E. Schooler)

The Kid Who Loved Christmas (film)

The Whole Life Adoption Book: Realistic Advice for Building a Healthy Adoptive Family (Jayne E. Schooler and Thomas C. Atwood)

The Year Dolly Parton Was My Mom (film)

Three Little Words (Ashley Rhodes-Courter)

The Birth Order Book: Why You Are The Way You Are (Dr. Kevin Leman)

Twenty Life Transforming Choices Adoptees Need to Make (Sherrie Eldridge)

Twenty Things Adopted Kids Wish Their Adoptive Parents Knew (Sherrie Eldridge)

Resources for Kids:

Adoption Is For Always (Linda Walvoord Girard)

All About Adoption: How Families Are Made and How Kids Feel About It (Mark A. Neimiroff and Jane Annuziata)

Did My First Mother Love Me? (Kathryn Ann Miller)

Flora's Family (Annette Aubrey)

How I Was Adopted (Joanna Cole)

I Don't Have Your Eyes (Carrie A Kitze)

Is That Your Sister? (Catherine and Sherry Bunin)

Let's Talk About Adoption (Fred Rogers)

My Family is Forever (Nancy Carlson)

Oliver: A Story About Adoption (Lois Wickstrom)

Star of the Week: A Story of Love, Adoption, and Brownies with Sprinkles (Darlene Friedman)

The Secret of Me (Meg Kearney)

The Willoughbys (Lois Lowry)

True Colors (Natalie Kinsey Warnock)

CHAPTER TEN

"Are They Real Siblings?": Life as a Growing Adoptive Family

"We are not only our brother's keeper; in countless large and small ways, we are our brother's maker."

~BONARO OVERSTREET

"I don't believe an accident of birth makes people sisters or brothers. It makes them siblings, gives them mutuality of parentage. Sisterhood and brotherhood is a condition people have to work at."

~MAYA ANGELOU

As you prepare to add to your family through adoption, you must keep in mind that every child-parent relationship and every adoption is unique. Adoptive parents must enter into adoptions without letting their past experiences bestow unrealistic expectations upon their next child and his or her adoption.

181

What worked for one child may not work for another. You might have two totally different adoptions: perhaps one will be open, and one will be closed. Maybe one child has special needs while the other is one hundred percent healthy. Or perhaps your current children are biological and you are preparing to adopt for the first time.

Are We Ready To Adopt (Again)?

Choosing to expand your family through adoption can be a nerve-wracking experience. Adoption is full of both an incredible amount of unknowns and of predictable challenges.

Before choosing to adopt for the first time or for a subsequent time, consider the following:

- *Your current financial situation.* Are your finances stable, or better yet, doing well? Have you secured funds for an adoption? Have you researched adoption costs and prepared yourself for possible additional expenses that might crop up due to an adoption specifically, but also those due to adding another child to your family?

- *Your current children.* Are any of your current children facing dire or particularly tough struggles right now? If so, are you seeking the appropriate assistance for your child at this time or are you in the searching-for-assistance stage? Are any of your children facing a great change currently or in the near-future, such as a major surgery, marriage, or heading to college? Do you have enough time and energy for the children you currently have?

- *Your relationship with your partner.* Is your relationship stable? Is your partner on board with adopting? What type of adoption? Are you both equally committed to the type of adoption you wish to pursue? Are you both pursuing adoption education?

- *Your home.* Is your home a place where you can accommodate another child in the way that is most beneficial for your current children and for the new child? Is your home located in an area that provides a school system with programs equipped to handle the needs of your future child and your current children? (A move can be upsetting for any child, but especially for the child who has been moved time and time again. A move is best done before the new child arrives).

- *Your job.* Do you have a job where you can take a leave of absence (paid or unpaid)? How would a leave affect your household finances?

- *Your health (mental, physical, emotional, spiritual).* Are you facing struggles in any health areas? How taxing are they on your everyday life and current parenting? Are you seeking treatment or counsel?

- *Your childcare arrangement.* Do you have a satisfactory childcare arrangement for your current and future children? Will you or your partner be able to take an extended leave of absence from work to foster healthy attachment with your new child and help your current children adjust to a sibling?

Preparing Children for a Sibling

Adoptive families should know that no matter how a child is brought into a family, there will be variances that should be appreciated and embraced. Arleta James, author of *Brothers and Sisters in Adoption*, explains, "Whether siblings are related by birth or by adoption, a variety of issues colors relationships, including general family culture and closeness, the sex of the children, their relative ages, their position in the family, the size of the family, similarity or disparity of interests and talents, individual children's personality styles, and each person's sense of 'psychological fit' within the family system" (511).

There is no how-to manual on flawlessly merging a child with the existing family, simply because it's not possible. However, you can take steps to prepare your children for a new sibling:

- Use resources, such as books or videos, to introduce the decision to adopt (especially transracially) and what that means. Continue using resources to discuss adoption.

- Join an all-family adoption support group and socialize with other adoptive families.

- Include the children in the process. Take them to meetings with social workers or attorneys and allow them to ask questions. Let them help you organize adoption paperwork.

- Set up your new child's room and allow your children to help. Tasks might include painting, putting together furniture, folding clothes, organizing books and toys, picking out décor.

- Place an empty chair at the table and talk about the new sibling who will sit there. If you include a meal-time prayer, pray for the child who will fill the empty chair. Likewise, place the new child's car seat in the car.

- Give each child a camera to take pictures of whatever he or she desires: favorite things, steps in the adoption process, etc. Create a photo book for the family or for the new child. Drawings and letters can be added to it, too.

- Gather or purchase dolls or figurines of various races. Play with your children, showing them that people can look different and be a family.

- Spend time with your children individually. Ask them about how they feel about adoption and if they have questions. Likewise, spend time with your children without discussing adoption (unless, of course, the child brings it up); focus instead on the child and his or her current joys, challenges, and accomplishments. Establish that your relationship with your child will be of continued importance, even after the new child arrives.

Nesting...Again

Whether your current children are biologically yours, are adopted, or are a mix of both, you probably went through a nesting period prior to their arrival. Now it's time to nest again!

As a family grows, so do your responsibilities. As you nest, consider preparing for your growing family by:

- Making and freezing meals.

- Stocking up on items the child and your family will need (clothing, toiletries, groceries, medications, etc.) to minimize trips to the store.

- "Spring" cleaning.

- Setting home maintenance appointments to avoid service calls after the new child arrives.

- Setting doctor, dentist, and other appointments such as physicals, yearly exams, and follow-up appointments.

- Setting up online bill paying to avoid unnecessary trips to the post office.

- Interviewing and hiring help: house cleaner, landscaper, babysitter, tutor, etc.

- Contacting potential resources (and possibly making appointments) for the future child so you have their information on hand when the child arrives.

- Researching travel costs (hotel, car rental, airfare, etc.) involved in bringing your child home.

- Working ahead on any projects or research you are involved with at your place of employment.

- Setting up and organizing your new child's room; rearranging bedroom situations as necessary with your current children.

- Continuing to read about adoption, attending your support group meetings, and talking with your adoption mentor.

- Researching and seeking support in areas specific to your future child: newborn care, medical issues, renovations to your home to accommodate a child with a disability, etc.

Anticipating Post-Adoption Challenges

Children thrive on predictability and routine, so they will naturally face some challenges when a new sibling enters the home. Jayne E. Schooler and Thomas C. Atwood describe eight challenges children might face (98-110) and strategies to combat them:

- "Changing the Birth Order"
- "Children May Witness Distress, Sadness, and Anger When the Family Struggles"

- "New Behavior Management (Discipline) Techniques and House Rules"

- "Children May Believe Their Opinions and Feelings Don't Matter"

- "Children May Feel Tricked Into Supporting the Adoption"

- "Parents May Regret or Feel Guilty About the Adoption"

- "Children May Have to Explain to Friends and Schoolmates About Adoption"

- "Children May Become Invisible to Their Parents After the Adoption of a Child With Special Needs"

Some families embrace a new child almost seamlessly, while other families face several of these challenges. I encourage you to explore these topics in more depth by reading Schooler and Atwood's book.

Likewise, adoptive families should keep in mind that if they are transforming into a transracial family, current children might face struggles, such as questions from relatives, teasing from peers, and personal confusion, as well. Adoptive parents should ask their children directly how they feel about transracial adoption and openly discuss and seek to resolve any obstacles that may arise.

Once your child is home, it's wise to have a family meeting in which you revise or create a disclosure plan. What information may children readily share with family members, friends, and strangers? What information is to be kept private? A clear plan will help your children feel more confident and empowered instead of confused when questions about the newly adopted child arise.

Keeping Up While Staying and Getting Connected

Whether preparing to adopt for the first time or the tenth time, adoptive families raising multiple children face the challenge of nurturing their current children while also forming a healthy attachment with the new child.

Shirley Crenshaw, MSW, LCSW, shares that each child in the home requires "an incredible amount of time." She notes to say that some adoptive children need as much attention as a newborn which can over-extend any parent, especially one who is already caring for multiple other children. In fact, a fellow adoptive mom had shared with me that her child's therapist said that parenting an adopted child can be the equivalent of parenting three (biological) children (depending, of course, on the child's history and current struggles). Crenshaw offers these suggestions:

- *Be present.* If possible, take a leave of absence from work and be the children's primary caregiver for a significant period. Newly adopted children shouldn't be forced to go "Mommy shopping" or "Daddy shopping" from a selection of caregivers who are not the child's parents.

- *Date.* Crenshaw suggests that parents carve out dates with each child to give him or her full time and attention. Against what might appear to be common sense, Crenshaw says that during the adjustment period, children need less family time and more one-on-one attention from the parent(s).

- *Accept help.* Being a mom or dad to a newly adopted child can be incredibly exhausting. Shirley suggests that parents allow well-intended relatives and friends to help in practical ways: they can wash and fold laundry, prepare meals, mow the lawn, and so on. That way, mom or dad has more time and energy to focus on the children. If parents can afford it, ongoing hired-help for lawn mowing, housecleaning, or tutors for the kids can be beneficial.

- *Empathize.* Current children might feel left-out as the new child soaks up the attention and energy of not just the parents but also relatives, friends, and neighbors. Parents should frequently check in with their children and, as previously suggested, engage in individual dates with the children instead of insisting on family time. Obtain books from the suggested resources at the end of this chapter and explore them with your children.

- *Be prepared.* As the honeymoon period (the initial time after your child comes home) wears off, struggles and challenges begin to come forth. Arleta James writes, "The demands for intimacy and full participation as brother and sister, son or daughter are limited" initially, but "as the adoptee begins to comprehend that the placement is permanent" (as does the rest of the family) changes begin to take place (293). Have resources, such as professional help, available to assist your family as the honeymoon period ceases.

And Then There's You and Your Significant Other

In chapter 3, I discussed avenues of self-care and the importance of staying connected with your partner. When more children are added to the family, the family's stress level naturally increases, and self-care and marital maintenance become even more important. A newly adopted child who has special needs can increase stress even more. For example, my father works with autistic families; he has found that the divorce rate of parents with autistic children hovers at well over eighty percent. It takes an extraordinary amount of patience and unity for a marriage to succeed in the face of extreme challenges.

When a new child comes into the home, there is often a honeymoon period in which life seems to be going very well. You are perhaps surrounded by family and friends who are bringing gifts and meals. Your child is receiving lots of attention from both those you know and those you don't—the general public. This period can be a glorious and exhilarating time for adoptive parents. The child might seem to be adjusting quite well. However, as the honeymoon period gives way to everyday life, the attention wanes and the child begins to exhibit emotions and actions that demonstrate his or her past and present struggles and the other children in the family face challenges as they adapt. In such circumstances, parents often give themselves completely to the children, neglecting their marriage and their personal own personal needs.

All parents—biological or adoptive—face seasons of struggle, both personally and in their relationships. What we choose to do about them can have a forever-impact on ourselves, our relationships, and on our family as a whole. When these tough times come about, as they inevitably will, parents need to assess the situation and take reasonable and immediate actions to keep the family, their marriage, and their individual selves on track. Don't allow your selflessness to become selfish.

Questions from the Trenches

Strangers are always pointing out the differences between my children's skin colors. I'm not sure what their point is or how I should respond.

I understand! My oldest daughter is medium-brown, whereas my youngest daughter, particularly in the summer when she is more tanned, is dark, dark brown. Strangers are always asking us if the girls have the same mom (um, yes—me!), or they will say regarding my youngest, "She is sooooo dark." We've also been asked if each girl is "full" or "mixed."

Colorism is still alive and well today. Society says that the lighter you are, the prettier, more accepted, more successful, and less threatening you are. This attitude seems to contradict our society's obsession with tanning; however, let's remember that skin color is often more about racial stereotypes and prejudices than it is about physical color. As I've noted in previous chapters, skin color ties a person to a racial community and culture, and in America, despite the progress our nation has made, the darker-skinned you are, the more you are to be feared, questioned, and considered untrustworthy.

There's also, I've noticed, a greater acceptance of adoptive families who adopt darker-skinned children from outside the United States. These children are seen to be more exotic (and perhaps more deserving of being adopted) than children of the same skin color who are adopted domestically. A common question we get is, "What country are the girls from?" There is almost always a bit of disappointment in the stranger's eyes when we say, "the United States." There's a common belief that orphans only live outside of the United States; this is your opportunity, if you so choose, to explain that there are over a hundred thousand children in our country who are free for adoption right now through the foster care system. What many people do not understand is that Black birth moms often have very few adoptive families to choose from, whereas a White birth mom might have dozens of families willing to adopt her infant. You might choose to explain this as well, depending on the situation and whether your children are present or not.

No matter how a skin color question or comment comes up, I have found that the best response is, "Aren't they both so beautiful?" Or, "Yes, we have two handsome boys!" Since it's likely that your children are with you when you are asked a question or a comment is made about their skin tones, you want to be sure to respond in a way that demonstrates to your children that they are equally valued and loved.

I have a biological child and a transracially adopted child. Sometimes people assume that my Black child is my other child's friend or that I'm babysitting. When a person learns that my children are siblings, a slew of questions begin. The most uncomfortable questions involve the words "real" or "my own" (referring to my biological child) while my other child is labeled as "adopted." How to I respond?

The simplest way to respond to questions and comments about the authenticity of your children and the level at which they are "real," is to stop the conversation from going further (and becoming more damaging). It's perfectly appropriate to say, "They are both my children" and change the subject or walk away from the conversation.

Remember, society generally views adoptive families as less-than and a second-class. The fact that you have a biological child sends a stranger's mind reeling. *Why didn't you have more biological children? How can you possibly love a child who is adopted as much as a child who is your biological offspring? How can these two kids, who look nothing alike and do not share genes, possibly be "real" siblings?* This could be the person's first encounter with a transracial adoptive family. Granted, your children didn't ask to be the poster children for adoption, so despite the person's motives, you have to respond in a way that is respectful of your children and their feelings.

If the person persists in asking questions or making comments, you can hand them one of your adoption agency's business cards and say, "You seem to want to know more about adoption. Here's my adoption agency's information."

I feel that I adequately prepared my children for a new sibling, yet when our new child arrived, our other children acted out in various way: tantrums, defiant behaviors, and sometimes even acting like babies themselves! I'm feeling torn between bonding with my new baby and dealing with the needs of the other children.

Adding a child to your family is a major change—one that your other children didn't ask for and likely didn't realistically anticipate, even though you worked to prepare them. Though adoptive parents like to picture adding children to their family as a butterflies-and-rainbows experience, one full of euphoria, the newness quickly wears off as everyone settles into real life.

Each of your children will handle the addition of the baby differently, and each is likely to face different struggles. Maybe one child has been teased at school for having a Black sibling while another is struggling with all the attention the baby is getting from Grandma. If this is your first transracially adopted child, strangers will give the baby loads of attention (even when it's unwelcome and uninvited), forcing your other children to feel displaced and insecure. Maybe one child is upset because the new sibling has an open adoption while his or her adoption is closed.

As difficult as it is, you must carve out time to focus on each individual child. Maybe you'll have date nights with each child or develop a new bedtime routine where kids get one-on-one attention with you or your partner. Work special times with your children into your calendar. Take advantage of those who offer to help you by allowing them to bring you meals, help with chores or errands, and occasionally provide childcare.

Additionally, do not neglect your own needs. When you spend all your time giving, it's easy to forget that to be the best parent possible, you need to nourish yourself physically, mentally, emotionally, and spiritually. Remember what they tell you when you're flying? In case of an emergency, put the oxygen mask on yourself first so that you can best serve the child sitting next to you.

We had a match fall through, and I'm not sure how to break the news to my children. They were so excited to have a new brother!

A failed match or referral is difficult for the entire adoptive family. Though you might be processing your own feelings of loss, confusion, and anger, do not delay talking to your children. It's best that they hear the news from you and not a family member or friend.

Sharing the news with your children is easier when you have been open about adoption from the very beginning of your process, approaching adoption with honesty, education, and communication. You may have already told your children that a match or referral isn't a guaranteed placement.

With children of any age, it's best to be direct and honest. There is no need to proceed with a complicated explanation, especially if your children are fairly young. Let the children know how you are feeling about the situation, and continue to be honest as your feelings evolve. Also, let the children know what will happen next. Are you back in the waiting game? Are you taking a break from waiting? Encourage your children to talk about their feelings.

For yourself, consider whether you are prepared to wait for another child or if a break from waiting is in order. Discuss your options with your adoption professional, and seek the support and encouragement that your support group, mentor, or counselor can offer.

We have a large, "rainbow" family, and people often make joking comments about the number of children we have, their various races, and the fact that we remind them of a celebrity family who keeps adopting their own "United Nations." These comments are

hurtful, and I especially worry about what impact they will have on our children. How can I respond?

Large families enthrall the public. Popular television shows like *Jon & Kate Plus 8* and *19 Kids and Counting* feed our curiosity and polarize our opinions. Reality television shows have grown to become a historical marking and ever-increasingly popular phenomenon. The common person can "friend" or "follow" celebrities on social media sites. Access to the lives of celebrities encourages Americans to judge not only those celebrities' choices, but one another's choices as well.

Your family already faces adoptism and racism, and now you face an additional form of prejudice: sizeism. People see the family as a parade to be watched, and many forget that each of your children are listening to and learning from the responses your family receives. I find that curiosity tends to replace common sense, and people ask insensitive and nosy questions that can be hurtful to my children.

Personally, I prefer to respond in a positive way — one that doesn't evoke shame or confusion in the children. You might say, "Yes we are a big family! You should see my grocery bill!" Or you can simply say, "Thank you" (even if the comment wasn't a compliment). You can even say something a bit silly such as, "We are loud and proud!" Remember that no matter your personality (sassy, sarcastic, introverted, etc.), you must respond in a way that honors your entire family.

There is no reason to fuel the curiosity and prejudice of strangers, or even friends or family members. Your primary responsibility is to the well-being of your children. You might, depending on your children's ages, have a discussion with them about comments people make, their feelings about such comments, and appropriate responses.

My adoption support group discussed this very issue, and some of us postulated that some people make comments because they personally feel guilty for not adopting. They might be dealing with feelings of jealousy or selfishness which prompts them to say something inappropriate and hurtful, disguised as a joke. It might surprise you that someone who has had the opportunity to have biological kids (and perhaps did so) would be jealous of an adoptive family, as society generally perpetuates adoptist (less-than, second-class) attitudes; however, it can happen. Depending on your relationship with the person making sarcastic (and/or passive-aggressive) comments, you might be wise to address the issue directly by telling the person that such comments are hurtful and offensive to both you and your entire family, and, of course, can be harmful to the well-being of your children.

Questions for Further Discussion

- Review the "Are We Ready to Adopt (Again)?" section of this chapter. In what areas are you ready to adopt? What areas need work before (or as you proceed into) an adoption?

- In what ways can you prepare your child(ren) for a sibling?

- How can you nest now to best serve your family later?

- What support systems do you have in place to combat post-adoption challenges with your newly adopted child, your current children, your spouse, and yourself?

- How can you prepare now for keeping connected with your current children once your new child arrives?

- In what ways do you plan to stay connected with your partner once the new child arrives?

Practical Application

To prepare your child(ren) for a new sibling, watch *Stuart Little* (1999) as a family. Discuss the challenges that Stuart's big brother, George, and Snowbell, the family cat, faced as they adjusted to the addition of a new family member. Emphasize to your children that change can be confusing and difficult, even when it is positive, and establish that there will be ongoing and honest communication about siblinghood, race, and adoption in your household.

To emphasize the importance of children having as sibling who looks like them, watch the film *The Muppets* (2011). Observe how Walter (who is physically very different from his older brother Walter) pursues connecting with those who look like him and how he feels, at times, when the connection isn't made.

Resources for Parents

Brothers and Sisters in Adoption: Helping Children Navigate Relationships When New Kids Join the Family (Arleta James)

The Sibling Effect: What the Bonds Among Brothers and Sisters Reveal About Us (Jeffrey Kluger)

Resources for Kids

Note: Some of these resources are not adoption-themed, rather, they are sibling-themed to help children navigate a new sibling entering into the family.

All Together Now (Anita Jeram)

Arthur: Big Brother Binky (DVD)

Barfburger Baby, I Was Here First (Paula Danziger)

Brand-New Baby Blues (Kathi Appeit)

But I Wanted a Baby Brother! (Kate Feiffer and Diane Goode)

Chloe, Instead (Micah Player)

Dinosaur Train: Buddy's World

Dinosaur Train: Dinosaur Big City (DVD)

Emma Dilemma: Big Sister Poems (Kristine O'Connell George)

Emma's Yucky Brother (Jean Little)

Friends and Pals and Brothers, Too (Sarah Wilson)

I'm Your Peanut Butter Big Brother (Selina Alko)

Is That Your Sister?: A True Story of Adoption (Catherine and Sherry Bunin)

Little Brown Bear and the Bundle of Joy (Jane Dyer)

Look at Me! (Rachel Fuller)

Love That Baby! (Karen Lasky)

One Special Day: A Story for Big Brothers & Sisters (Lola M. Schaefer)

Peter's Chair (Ezra Jack Keats)

Sophie Peterman Tells the Truth! (Sarah Weeks)

Stuart Little (DVD)

Vera's Baby Sister (Vera Rosenberry)

Waiting for May (Janet Morgan Stoeke)

Whoa, Baby, Whoa! (Grace Nichols)

CHAPTER ELEVEN

Where's the Black?: Supporting Your Transracially Adopted Child

"I don't think much of a man who is not wiser than he was yesterday."

~ABRAHAM LINCOLN

"There is only one good, knowledge, and one evil, ignorance."

~SOCRATES

One thing that has been particularly helpful for our family is recognizing that it's not "them" (the kids, who were adopted and who are Black) and "us" (the parents, who are White), but "we." We are a transracial family, a, White/Black, Black/White unit. Therefore, the racial culture that our children brought to our family merges with the racial culture our family already possessed. Combined, we have a single identity composed of merged traditions, backgrounds, and experiences. Our children do not have to navigate being Black/White alone, because we are immersed in the process together.

Granted, you can tell your children that your family stands together as one, but "the proof is in the pudding." Demonstrate, using strategies provided in this chapter, that you are honestly committed to continuously merge your two (or more) racial cultures within your family.

Transracial adoptive parenting is an ongoing, progressive action. We cannot simply purchase a Black baby doll for our child and own one book on Jackie Robinson, and then sit back and congratulate ourselves on a job well done. I provide you with a plethora of options on how to encourage your child to learn more about his or her racial culture.

I am not suggesting that parents abandon all traditions and family culture that existed before the child came into the family. In fact, part of belonging to a family occurs when the child engages in established family traditions and culture. However, as with any part of transracial adoptive parenting, adoptive parents should consider recreating and modifying the family's culture to meet the needs of the transracially adopted child. Remember, the world will always see your child as a person of color. The child will, for a time, be able to live under the White umbrella; however, as he or she grows up and spends more time away from you, the child will need to have an understanding of and confidence in his or her racial identity.

Why Is a Focus on Race Important?

Parents may experience the world as not particularly racist and think that race isn't a big deal. Some parents may be in denial that race *is* a big deal, and others may be uncomfortable about discussing and dealing with race even though they choose to adopt transracially. Many people (including myself when we first started our adoption journey) know little about other racial cultures and traditions; therefore, they feel lost trying to explore these with their children.

Deborah D. Gray, author of *Attaching in Adoption: Practical Tools for Today's Parents*, asked adult transracial adoptees what they would say about children in their situation (157):

- "They want to be raised in a community that has others of their same race."

- "They want to feel comfortable with traditions, attitudes, and people of their own race."

- "They experienced love and acceptance, but were sometimes hurt by 'color-blind' attitudes of their parents."

- "People of the same race can expose and transmit attitudes and traditions from within a family context."

- "Instead of talking about racial issues, children see them modeled. When parents cannot model, they have to find other ways to help their children to feel competent and esteemed as a minority person in the culture."

Black History Month

We choose to celebrate Black History Month, which is each February, in our home because we believe that putting an emphasis on Black leaders empowers and educates our family. Martin Luther King's famous "I Have a Dream" speech reminds us why civil rights leaders put their lives on the line; I encourage families to watch, listen to, or read King's speech. Though Black History Month is assigned a single month, these activities may be carried out throughout the year:

- Watch films that celebrate the hardships and triumphs of Blacks.
- Read books about Black leaders and Black history.
- Listen to music by some of the great Black artists.

- Visit a monument, cemetery, historical home, or park that has significance to Black history.

- Attend a festival, art show, museum exhibit, or parade that celebrates Blacks.

- Do crafts that connect to lessons from Black history.

- Make a traditional soul food meal or a meal reflective of your child's racial culture.

- Write a letter of appreciation to a Black leader. Younger kids can draw or color a picture.

- Purchase books, music, and films that feature Blacks and donate them to your local school or public library.

- Support Black-owned businesses: restaurants, stores, salons, and so on.

Use your child's current interests to jumpstart your Black History Month celebration, and do your research. If your child likes country music, for example, listen to music by Black country music artists such as Darius Rucker or Charlie Pride. If your child has an interest in baking, make stoplight cookies (rectangular cookies, each with a row of one red, one, yellow, and one green chocolate candy, placed vertically, to celebrate Garrett Morgan, inventor of what is now the modern-day stoplight. If your child has an interest in transportation like my children, talk about Rosa Parks and her contribution to the bus boycotts. Be creative, and enjoy learning!

Parents shouldn't limit themselves to learning about Black history. It's important to educate yourself on current Black culture and the issues that concern Blacks as well. Suggestions include subscribing to Black magazines such as *Jet*, *Ebony*, and *Essence* and checking in with websites like *The Huffington Post*, which features a page called "Black Voices." For me, it's been valuable to learn about Black issues and culture from the perspectives of Blacks.

Kwanzaa

The official Kwanzaa website states: "Kwanzaa is an African American and Pan-African holiday which celebrates family, community and culture. Celebrated from 26 December thru 1 January, its origins are in the first harvest celebrations of Africa from which it takes its name. The name Kwanzaa is derived from the phrase 'matunda ya kwanza' which means 'first fruits' in Swahili, a Pan-African language which is the most widely spoken African language." The website further explains that Kwanzaa isn't a religious celebration but is instead a cultural celebration.

The seven principles of Kwanzaa (one celebrated per day) are: unity, self-determination, collective work and responsibility, cooperative economics, purpose, creativity, and faith.

You can use the previous suggestions for celebrating Black History Month as ways to celebrate Kwanzaa as well. Some organizations host local Kwanzaa celebrations. Adoptive parents who choose to celebrate Kwanzaa in their household can take advantage of resources that offer suggestions on Kwanzaa attire, crafts, music, food, and gifts.

Juneteenth

According to Juneteenth.com, "Juneteenth is the oldest nationally celebrated commemoration of the ending of slavery in the United States. From its Galveston, Texas origin in 1865, the observance of June 19th as the African American Emancipation Day has spread across the United States and beyond."

As the website states, Juneteenth celebrations are not (and should not be) limited to Blacks. Juneteenth marks a significant time in history that has impacted the lives of all Americans. The website also offers suggestions for celebrating this holiday in your workplace, in your community, and in your home.

National Adoption Month

National Adoption Month is held each November. Its primary purpose is to call attention the one-hundred-thousand-plus children who are waiting in the domestic foster care system for forever families. However, many adoptive families also celebrate adoption in general during November.

Patricia Irwin Johnston, author of *Adoption Is a Family Affair!: What Relatives and Friends Must Know*, offers several suggestions on ways to celebrate Adoption Month, including inviting a birth mother or adoption professional to lunch to show your compassion and appreciation. Other suggestions include asking your local library to purchase favorite adoption titles for the library. (Our family has asked our local libraries to create special adoption displays for the month of November.) Johnston also suggests offering to host a traveling adoptive family in your home or becoming a foster family (134-135).

If your family is not pursuing foster care adoption but you wish to assist children in the foster care system, you can celebrate National Adoption Month by contacting a local foster-care non-profit organization, Department (of Child and) Family Services, or group home and ask how you can serve (be it through volunteering, collecting items, or mentoring a child).

Culture Camps

Arleta James, author of *Brothers and Sisters in Adoption*, shares, "At culture camps, also called heritage camps, adoptees have the rare chance to be in the majority. Culture camps seek to familiarize children with culture of origin. They do so by introducing them to the country's music, art, traditions, holidays, clothing, language, food, history, and so on" (438). Many adoptive parents I have interviewed claim that attending culture camp is the highlight of their family's year, and many of these families make culture camp their yearly vacation. James points out, "For culture camp to be effective, it needs to be extended beyond the camp experience.

That is, culture camps should be considered one way adoptive parents facilitate the positive identity development of their transcultural adoptee and entire family for that matter" (438). For a list of camps, visit *Adoptive Families* magazine's webpage and click on the "Celebrating Heritage" link.

Racial Role Models

I discussed racial role models in chapter 8. If you haven't yet taken steps to befriend individuals of your child's race, now is the time to do so. One suggestion is to contact your local university and ask to be connected with a student organization or faculty member who might be able to put you in communication with potential racial role models for your child. For example, one program at the university where I teach works with many African American students. I called the program's director, and she was able to recommend one of her student workers as a potential candidate (as a mentor for my daughters). I also contacted the leader of our school's gospel choir, and she recommended four young ladies. Steve and I conducted interviews and chose one young lady to hire. She comes to our home once a week and plays with our daughters.

Before choosing a mentor, I recommend creating a list of qualifications. For us, we wanted a Black, female college student who was a Christian, confident, patient, supportive of transracial adoption, and experienced in working with children. When interviewing candidates, we directly asked them what they thought about adoption and transracial adoption. We asked their future educational and career goals, and, of course, their availability. Be clear what you are willing to pay (or is it voluntary?) and what you expect of the person when he or she is interacting with your children. Due to our adoption processes, we also told the candidates that they would potentially be asked to submit to a background check. (This provides them with the opportunity to state if they have had any criminal history.)

If your child is younger and you are a mother, you can research joining a local Mocha Moms group. Take steps now to broaden your circle of friends and embrace people of your child's race.

Cultural Hot Spots

You may not have to travel far to find cultural hot spots where your family can participate in your child's racial culture. Whether you are staying near home or going on vacation, you should make efforts to learn more about your child's racial culture and engage in it. Consider:

- Restaurants

- Shops

- Monuments and historical locations

- Festivals and parades

- Performances

- Exhibits

Everyday Fun

Incorporating your child's racial culture in your everyday life is as simple as purchasing items (or borrowing them from the library, or creating them yourself) and having them in your home as an option for daily play. Remember that you want to emphasize diversity so your child can learn an appreciation for others not just those of their own race, but people of all races. Try these:

- Games (board, electronic, computer, card, and apps): a good one is eeBoo's I Never Forget a Face! Matching Game

- Music: CDS from the Putumayo Kids-series, such as *African Playground*

- Books: as I listed in this book

- Toys: dolls or action figures, puzzles, etc.

- Movies: as I listed in this book

- Art: Create a wall collage of prints that feature brown-skinned people. Use postcards, custom-created prints, pages from books, posters, etc.

- Meals: Make and serve a soul food meal. Whether you are a meat-eater, vegetarian, or vegan, there are many cookbooks and online recipes to inspire you.

Filling the Gap

Parents and their children may notice that the places they frequent (school, their place of worship, or the places where they take part in extracurricular activities) do not feature resources (books, music, movies, art, magazines, toys) that reflect diversity. Likewise, publications created by such institutions, such as newsletters, websites, or other promotional materials, lack diverse photographs or politically correct language. This is more likely in areas where Blacks were once (or maybe still are) seen in a very negative light or where the population is composed mostly of Whites.

It's up to the parents or the children (if old enough) to articulate concerns about gaps in resources and publications to teachers, leaders, and committees. The other (or additional) option is to take action.

Join committees or start one, purchase materials to donate, volunteer to care for a certain task, or offer to help make changes. Action might be necessary to not only broaden diversity awareness, but to make it a topic of conversation in the first place.

I understand that funds can be extraordinarily limited, especially in poorer areas and during tough economic times, for many institutions and individuals. This is why it's important that parents understand what funds, if any, are available for purchasing resources and encouraging their institution to allocate a portion of those funds to filling in the gap. But if funds aren't available, parents should take it upon themselves to fill the gap. Strike a deal with a local bookstore, purchase gently used items, and volunteer to help implement changes that do not require money. For example, you can volunteer to help your child's teacher conduct Black History Month lessons and activities in the classroom.

As parents, it's easy for us to be so focused on our own children that we forget that our efforts to instill a healthy racial identity and confidence in them can reach beyond them. When we adopt transracially, we accept the unique task of educating ourselves, and our children, and those around us.

Questions from the Trenches

I'm incredibly frustrated with the lack of brown-skinned dolls available. When I do find Black dolls, their hair is often straight, long, and silky, unlike typical Black hair. Are there any companies out there who make dolls that realistically look like a Black girl?

I share in your frustration! Not only do many "Black" dolls feature White-girl hair, but they often have Euro-centric features and light-brown skin, which doesn't represent many Black girls. I have even found brown-skinned dolls that are supposedly Black, yet the dolls feature blond or light brown hair!

I have managed to find some dolls that share my girls' skin tones and feature natural hair. Many times, "ethnic" dolls are found on clearance aisles which is disheartening in one sense but also financially rewarding (more for your money!). I suggest that you be on the lookout for toys, books, and movies that feature brown-skinned kids when you are out shopping. You can always put these items away for later gift-giving occasions (including as gifts for friends' and cousins' birthday parties).

Some diversity-minded companies that I enjoy purchasing products from include: eeBoo (games, cards, etc.), American Girl (dolls and books), Pottery Barn Kids (dolls, Christmas stockings, bedding, etc.), Putumayo (CDs), Melissa and Doug (toys, games, art supplies, etc.), Corolle (dolls), Fisher-Price (Little People toys), and Jump at the Sun (books). I also suggest shopping on Etsy. com, where many sellers will create custom products if they do not already feature brown-skinned toys or art. Another option is to talk to managers at your favorite brick-and-mortar stores about broadening their selection of products to include kids of different races and skin-colors.

We are friends with another transracial adoptive family that doesn't incorporate their child's race into the child's life at all. The child seems to be perfectly content and healthy. I'm wondering if my efforts to merge White and Black culture in my home is putting too much emphasis on race. Am I going to give my child a complex?

I highly suggest that you read *In Their Own Voices: Transracial Adoptees Tell Their Stories* by Rita J. Simon and Rhonda M. Rhoorda. The authors interviewed dozens of transracial adoptees, many of whom were deeply burdened and hurt by their parents' lack of incorporation and knowledge of Black culture within the family unit. The adoptee's feelings of resentment, displeasure, confusion, and frustration wasn't always present when the child was younger, but in the teenage and adult years, the adoptee recognized a deep need to belong to people within his or her own racial community. The consensus I drew from the adoptees' stories is that parents who shy away from fostering their child's racial identity end up being scarred in one or more ways, which can cripple them in different areas of life.

The transracial adoptive parent community is fairly small, and we gauge our success against those few other transracial adoptive parents whom we know. However, some adoptees cannot articulate their emotions, and they are not always aware of why they are feeling lonely, discontent, or confused. This isn't to say that all children who are raised in a transracial adoptive family that doesn't foster racial identity end up being dysfunctional, insecure adults. Each child and every adoption is unique. However, armed with knowledge you have and from the numerous other resources I have listed, I encourage you to continue incorporating your child's racial culture into your family life.

As you lead your child and your family as a whole, take time to carefully examine how much and what type of emphasis you are placing on race. Negative? Realistic? Encouraging? Overwhelming? You know your child best. Evaluate what is working and what isn't, and make necessary changes along the way. And consider what Jayne E. Schooler and Thomas C. Atwood, authors of *The Whole Life Adoption Book: Realistic Advice for Building A Healthy Adoptive Family*, share: "[T]here is a sharp difference between recognizing and celebrating differences between child and parents and focusing on these differences too closely. Children may begin to feel isolated or alienated if racial and cultural differences are constantly stressed at the expense of their belonging to the family. Parents should realize that while some children will be very interested in learning more about their heritage from an early age, others may not have any interest at all" (73).

My daughter seems to only be interested in dating White boys. Likewise, the vast majority of her friends are White. I admit, I'm a bit disappointed. Did we do something wrong as her parents? Maybe we didn't do enough to teach her to be comfortable with those who share her race.

Marguerite A. Wright, author of *I'm Chocolate, You're Vanilla: Raising Healthy Black and Biracial Children in a Race-Conscious World* writes about parents purchasing same-race dolls for their young girls. She says that parents should allow their children to choose their dolls because, "I believe that it is but a short step from pressuring young children to choose only dolls that share their skin color to pressuring older children to choose only friends who are of their skin color" (53).

We do what we can for our children while they are young, offering them diverse opportunities and experiences, toys, and media. But children begin developing preferences at a very young age. Some newborns prefer to be held a certain way. Toddlers prefer certain foods over others. Grade-schoolers develop hobbies and talents and establish collections. It's no surprise that our children also have preferences for friends and dating partners.

As the parent, you see your daughter's choices in terms of race, which very well may play a part in her decisions—but what about the person's characteristics, values, and beliefs? It's quite possible your child is choosing friends and boyfriends based on commonalities and chemistry, not race.

All parents can look back and examine what they wish they had done differently or better, but you can't change the past. For another thing, even if you had done things differently (perhaps incorporated more Black culture into your child's life, for instance), there's still no guarantee that it would have changed your child's preferences for White friends and boyfriends. So my suggestion is this: go with the flow.

I was excited to learn that our local mall has both Black and White Santas. When I mentioned this to a friend, he exclaimed how ridiculous this was because everyone knows that Santa is White. Which Santa should I take my child to visit?

Yes, Santa has almost always been (and still is) represented as a White man. But Jesus is also depicted in most pictures as a White man, when it's very likely his skin was not milky-white but more likely a shade of brown. Matthew Ashimolowo writes in *What is Wrong With Being Black?* that despite popular belief and assumption, many Biblical figures were, in fact, brown-skinned (Black) people: Pharaoh's daughter (Moses' adoptive mother), Simon of Cyrene (who helped carry Jesus' cross), and Simon the Canaanite (one of the twelve apostles) (42-45).

It's evident to me that many Whites become defensive at suggestions that anything be portrayed outside the White norm because the idea that someone previously understood as White and great could actually be Black threatens White privilege and long-held beliefs. Your friend's reaction is not unusual. I often hear, "Why is there a Black History Month and not a White History Month?" His reaction is in-line with what society often says, orally or in policies and otherwise, about people of color: keep them down, tame, and in place.

What is more important than the decision to visit a Black or White Santa is the demonstration that your family is open to people of all races or colors. One friend of mine explains to her children that the Santa they see at the mall or at a holiday party isn't the real Santa, but is Santa's helper, and can be Black or White. The real Santa, the one who comes down the chimney and leaves presents, cannot be seen by children. And he, like Santa's helpers, can look any way the child imagines.

Questions for Further Discussion:

- Review the childhood "wants" listed by adult, transracial adoptees. In which areas are you currently succeeding as a parent? Which areas need examination and work?

- In what ways can you plan for your family to celebrate some traditional Black holidays? Begin planning and researching.

- Make a list of your child's current interests. What Black historical and current figures can you match with your child's interests?

- In what ways can your family celebrate National Adoption Month?

- Make a list of cultural hot spots in your area. Which ones do you plan to visit in the coming month?

- Take inventory of the Black resources, toys, art, and films in your home. What items are lacking?

- Where, as your child's parent, can you "fill the gap"?

Practical Application

Take your children out for ice cream. Order a chocolate cone, a vanilla cone, and a swirled (chocolate and vanilla) cone. Point out that before your children were adopted, you were separate entities. You were like the vanilla cone, and your children were like the chocolate cone. But when the adoption occurred, you and your children joined together to become ONE cone, the swirled cone, with your "colors" intricately intertwined.

Write a letter or e-mail of appreciation to a company that creates toys, games, or books that feature brown-skinned children. Let them know that you are thankful for their efforts to incorporate diversity into their playthings.

Resources for Parents

High on the Hog: A Culinary Journey From Africa to America (Jessica B. Harris)

Hog and Hominy: Soul Food From Africa to America (Frederick Douglass Opie)

Life Upon These Shores: Looking At African American History (Henry Louis Gates, Jr.)

Our Black Year: One Family's Quest to Buy Black in America's Racially Divided Economy (Maggie Anderson and Ted Gregory)

The Black Candle: A Kwanzaa Celebration (DVD)

The Healthy Soul Food Cook Book (Wilbert Jones)

The New Soul Food Cookbook for People with Diabetes (Fabiola Demps Gaines and Roniece Weaver)

The 100 Best African American Poems (Nikki Giovanni)

Resources for Kids on Blackness and Diversity

Beautiful Brown Eyes (Marianne Richmond)

Black Is Brown Is Tan (Arnold Adoff)

Black, White, Just Right! (Marguerite W. Davol)

Bright Eyes, Brown Skin (Cheryl Willis Hudson)

Brown Like Me (Noelle Lamperti)

Hands Around the World: 365 Creative Ways to Build Cultural Awareness and Global Respect (Susan Milord)

Heart and Soul: The Story of America and African Americans (Kadir Nelson)

I Like Myself! (Karen Beaumont)

Me I Am! (Jack Prelutsky)

Kids' Multicultural Cookbook: Food & Fun From Around the World (Deanna F. Cook)

My People (Langston Hughes)

Shades of Black (Sandra L. Pinkey)

Shades of People (Shelley Rotner)

The Colors of Us (Karen Katz)

The Crayon Box That Talked (Shane Derolf)

The Skin You Live In (Michael Tyler)

We Are the Ship: The Story of Negro League Baseball (Kadir Nelson)

Resources for Kids on Kwanzaa

Celebrating Kwanzaa (Diane Hoyt-Goldsmith)

Crafts for Kwanzaa (Kathy Ross)

Elmo's World: Happy Holidays (DVD)

K is for Kwanzaa: A Kwanzaa Alphabet Book (Juwanda G. Ford)

Kwanzaa Crafts (Carol Gnojewski)

My First Kwanzaa (Karen Katz)

Seven Candles for Kwanzaa (Andrea Davis Pinkney)

Seven Spools of Thread: A Kwanzaa Story (Angela Shelf Medearis)

The Gifts of Kwanzaa (Synthia Saint James)

The Sound of Kwanzaa (Dimitrea Tokunbo)

Resources for Kids on Christmas

Amazing Peace: A Christmas Poem (Maya Angelou)

An Island Christmas (Lynn Joseph)

Christmas Soul: African American Holiday Stories (Allison Samuels)

Grace at Christmas (Mary Hoffman)

Hold Christmas in Your Heart (Cheryl Willis Hudson)

Remember the Bridge: Poems of a People (Carole Boston Weatherford)

The Bells of Christmas (Virginia Hamilton)

'Twas the Night B'Fore Christmas: An African-American Version (Melodye Benson Rosales)

Under the Christmas Tree (Nikki Grimes)

Resources for Kids on Christianity

Children of God Storybook Bible (Archbishop Desmond Tutu)

God's Dream (Archbishop Desmond Tutu and Douglas Carlton Abrams)

He's Got the Whole World In His Hands (Kadir Nelson)

Jesus Loves the Little Children (Debbie Anderson)

Jubilee (Ellen Yeomans and Tim Ladwig)

The Jesus Storybook Bible (Sally Lloyd-Jones)

Resources for Kids on Black History

Note: There are numerous books on Black history. The resources I feature here provide a broad overview; I encourage you to seek resources on specific Black figures and movements by searching your local library's database. I often feature newly released Black history books on my blog: White Sugar, Brown Sugar.

The Hero in You (CD) (Ellis Paul)

A Kid's Guide to African American History: More Than 70 Activities (Nancy I. Sanders)

A Negro League Scrapbook (Carole Boston Weatherford)

Her Stories: African American Folktales, Fairy Tales, and True Tales (Virginia Hamilton)

Hip Hop Speaks to Children: A Celebration of Poetry With a Beat (edited by Nikki Giovanni)

How They Got Over: African Americans and the Call of the Sea (Eloise Greenfield)

I Lay My Stitches Down: Poems of African Slavery (Cynthia Grady)

Juneteenth Jamboree (Carole Boston Weatherford)

Jumping the Broom (Sonia W Black)

Our Children Can Soar: A Celebration of Rosa, Barack, and the Pioneers of Change (Michelle Cook)

The Beatitudes: From Slavery to Civil Rights (Carole Boston Weatherford)

What Color Is My World?: The Lost History of African-American Inventors (Kareem Abdul-Jabbar and Raymond Obstfeld)

CHAPTER TWELVE

Somewhere Over the Rainbow: What Tomorrow Might Bring

*"There is in this world no such force as the force of a person
determined to rise. The human soul cannot
be permanently chained."*

~W.E.B. DuBois

As a busy mom, I'm not a fan of the rain. It tends to put a damper on my daily to-do list which usually includes running several errands, entertaining my children, taking my oldest to and from school, and driving to the university to teach. Rain slows down my progress; it makes life move more slowly than I have the patience for.

One morning we awoke to gray, thick, looming clouds which soon released a steady downpour of rain. I was completely unmotivated to get myself and the kids out of our pajamas and head to the grocery store. We were all a bit restless, the rain having ruined any chance of playing on our swing set or going for a morning walk. The children were creating ways to entertain themselves, including taking toys away from each other and begging me, for the fiftieth time, to let them watch a movie.

My oldest came to me and piped up, "I have a good idea! Let's go outside!"

I sighed, wishing desperately for the rain to cease and the sun to come out. I replied, "It's raining, honey."

The toddler, having heard the words "go outside," was now at my side as well, her brown eyes imploring.

My oldest countered, "But we have rain boots, Mom!"

My gut reaction was to refuse the request. It was a bit chilly outside, I needed to load the dishwasher, and there were loads of clean laundry to fold. I needed to prepare my evening's lesson plans for work. But the desire to change our circumstances and uplift our moods triumphed.

We opened the hall closet and watched coats, scarves, mittens, and tote bags tumble onto the floor. I began digging through the pile to find what each person needed. We quickly dressed and headed toward the garage, umbrellas in hand.

As soon as the garage door lifted, the children were off to do what children do best: play. They twirled and jumped and skipped. They yelled. They threw their umbrellas in the air and clomped about in their too-big rain boots. My toddler smacked shallow water puddles, first carefully and then with great energy and purpose. They climbed a low tree, sang songs, and chased one another in circles. The oldest ordered us to line up behind her and then follow; we were to be the students and she would be the teacher, leading us about the schoolyard.

Somewhere in the midst of the adventures, the umbrellas were dropped to the ground and forgotten. They were too much of a hindrance.

Of course, it made sense to use an umbrella. That's what people do when it rains, right? We need to protect our clothes and hair and glasses and bags. We don't like getting and remaining wet. It's uncomfortable. But without the umbrella, we get to experience something new, something invigorating, something refreshing. When change is embraced, there is possibility.

Adopting my children has changed my life dramatically and for the better. Instead of dismissing someone who many claim "plays the race card," I consider what the person has to say, what experience led that individual to feeling less-than, preyed-upon, dehumanized. Instead of talking about "those people" as if they are aliens from another planet, I realize that the struggles of "those people" are my struggles, too. Instead of labeling people in terms of their race, I carefully consider, as Dr. King once said, the "content of their character." Instead of dismissing birth parents as irresponsible, heartless, promiscuous people, I have been drawn to those who have "lost" their children to adoption. Instead of calling children who were adopted "adopted kids," I look at them as children, first and foremost. Instead of defining family by biology, I define family by people who love, care about, and support one another.

In traveling "somewhere over the rainbow," in the continual walk into the bizarre, bittersweet, and complex journey of transracial adoption and parenting, in the midst of visiting my kids' birth families and speaking with prospective adoptive parents, and in learning who I am and what I can become, I've evolved into someone so much more than the person the world says I should be.

I hope that one day, adoptive families will be treated as equals to biological families. I hope that my children, and all other adoptees, will not be seen as either extraordinary or disabled because they were adopted, but will instead be viewed as people who can offer the world incredible gifts, talents, and insights which stem from the result of both the nature and nurture they have inherited and experienced. I hope that the stigmas and stereotypes surrounding adoption disintegrate, making room for diversity, acceptance, and friendship. I hope that someday it will not matter if parents and siblings and aunts and uncles and spouses "match" or not, but that will instead matter is the value and benefits and beauty of those relationships.

While we wait and yearn for a better tomorrow, let's not sit back and simply stew in anger or shrug our shoulders in indifference and ignorance. Create the world you want your children to behold. Empower yourself, empower others, embrace change, unlock mysteries, listen, share, teach, seek, ask, reflect, inspire. Live each day as an example to those around you. Stand tall. Stand firm. Be proud. Walk with confidence.

Above all, ditch the umbrella and dance in the rain with the children you have been chosen to love, nurture, and protect.

Works Cited

Note: Any page numbers listed after the following entries refer to the quotes presented at the beginning of the book chapter.

Prologue:

"Proverbs 24:3-4 NIV Version." *Bible Gateway*. Web. 30 Sept. 2012.

Chapter 1:

Eldridge, Sherrie. *Twenty Things Adopted Kids Wish Their Adoptive Parents Knew*. New York: Dell Publishing, 1999.

Johnston, Patricia Irwin. *Adoption is a Family Affair!: What Relatives and Friends Must Know*. Philadelphia: Jessica Kingsley Publishers, 2012.

Shaw, George Bernard. "Knowledge Quotes." *MotivatingQuotes*. Web. 31 Jul. 2012.

Watkins, Mary, and Susan Fisher, MD. *Talking with Young Children about Adoption*. New Haven: Yale University Press, 1993.

Wolff, Jana. *Secret Thoughts of an Adoptive Mother*. Honolulu: Vista Communications, 2000.

Chapter 2:

James, Arleta. *Brothers and Sisters in Adoption: Helping Children Navigate Relationships When New Kids Join the Family.* Indianapolis, Indiana: Perspectives Press, Inc., 2009. 41.

Johnston, Patricia Irwin. *Adoption is a Family Affair!: What Relatives and Friends Must Know.* Philadelphia: Jessica Kingsley Publishers, 2012.

Smith, Darron T., Cardell K. Jacobson, and Brenda G. Juarez. *White Parents, Black Children: Experiencing Transracial Adoption.* Lanham, Maryland: Rowman and Littlefield Publishers, Inc., 2011.

Chapter 3:

Crenshaw, Shirley. Personal interview. 24 Jul. 2012

Connell, Sara. *Bringing In Finn: An Extraordinary Surrogacy Story.* Berkeley, California: Seal Press, 2012. 245.

Foli, Karen J., PhD, and John R. Thompson, MD. *The Post-Adoption Blues: Overcoming the Unforeseen Challenges of Adoption.* United States: Rodale, 2004.

Gray, Deborah D. *Attaching in Adoption: Practical Tools for Today's Parents.* Indianapolis, Indiana: Perspectives Press, Inc., 2002.

Hormann, Elizabeth. *Breastfeeding and Adopted Baby and Relactation.* Schaumburg, IL: La Leche League International, 2006.

Johnston, Patricia Irwin. *Adoption is a Family Affair! What Relatives and Friends Must Know.* Philadelphia: Jessica Kingsley Publishers, 2012.

Kassing, Dee. Personal Interview. Oct. 2012.

Moss, Kathleen G. "What is Attachment?" *ATTACh.org.* Web. 31 Jul. 2012.

Sears, William, MD., and Martha Sears, RN. *The Attachment Parenting Book: A Commonsense Guide to Understanding and Nurturing Your Baby.* New York: Little, Brown, and Company, 2001.

Chapter 4:

Garlinghouse, Rachel. "Is PAL Too PC?" *Adoptive Families*. March/April 2012: 19.

O'Toole, Elisabeth. *In On It: What Adoptive Parents Would Like You To You Know About Adoption*. St. Paul, Minnesota: Fig Press, 2011.

Tatum, Beverly Daniel. *"Why Are All the Black Kids Sitting Together in the Cafeteria?": And Other Conversations About Race*. United States: Perseus Books Group, 1997.

Trager, Lauren. "Family Claims Discrimination at Little Rock Zoo." *KARK 4 NEWS*. 18 Mar. 2012. Web. 20 Aug. 2012.

Wolff, Jana. *Secret Thoughts of an Adoptive Mother*. Honolulu: Vista Communications, 2000. 74.

Chapter 5:

"atopic dermatitis (eczema)." *Mayo Clinic*. Web. 5 Jun. 2012.

Hadley, Rory. *Chocolate Hair, Vanilla Care*. Web.

"Mayo Clinic: Vitamin D's Link to Diseases Prevalent in Black Americans." *Mayo Clinic*. Web. 5 Jun. 2012.

van Gulden, Holly and Lisa M. Bartels-Rabb. *Real Parents, Real Children: Parenting the Adopted Child*. New York: Crossroad, 2000.

Chapter 6:

Foli, Karen J. and John R. Thompson. *The Post-Adoption Blues: Overcoming The Unforeseen Challenges Of Adoption*. United States: Rodale, 2004.

Keefer, Betsy, and Jayne E. Schooler. *Telling the Truth to Your Adopted or Foster Child: Making Sense of the Past*. Westport, Connecticut: Bergin & Garvey, 2000. 22.

Melina, Lois Ruskai and Sharon Kaplan Roszia. *The Open Adoption Experience*. New York: HarperPerennial, 1993.

O'Toole, Elisabeth. *In On It: What Adoptive Parents Would Like You to You Know About Adoption*. St. Paul, Minnesota: Fig Press, 2011.

Chapter 7:

Associated Press. "Black couple says racism forced wedding relocation." *CBS News*. 28 Jul. 2012. Web. 27 Aug. 2012.

Baldwin, Kristen. "Could this man be the first black Bachelor?" *Entertainment Weekly*. 30 Mar. 2012. Web. 27 Aug. 2012.

della Cava, Marco R. "George Lucas' 'Red Tails' salutes Tuskegee Airmen." *USA Today-Life*. 5 Jan. 2012. Web. 26 Aug. 2012.

Effron, Lauren. "Georgia School Investigates 'Slave' Math Problems." *ABC News-Nation*. 10 Jan. 2012. Web. 27 Aug. 2012.

Keefer, Betsy, and Jayne E. Schooler. *Telling the Truth to Your Adopted or Foster Child: Making Sense of the Past*. Westport, Connecticut: Bergin & Garvey, 2000.

King Jr., Dr. Martin Luther. "Martin Luther King Jr." *The Quotations Page*. Web. 29 Aug. 2012.

Parks, Rosa. "Rosa Parks." *The Quotations Page*. Web. 29 Aug. 2012.

Springer, Sarah. "'Scandal' updates image of black women on network television." *CNN-In America*. 25 May 2012. Web. 27 Aug. 2012.

"teacher forgets kids name, calls him 'black boy.'" *MSN-Now*. 9 June 2012. Web. 27 Aug. 2012.

Wright, Marguerite A. *I'm Chocolate, You're Vanilla: Raising Health Black and Biracial Children in a Race-Conscious World*. San Francisco: Jossey-Bass, 1998.

Chapter 8:

Gray, Deborah D. *Attaching in Adoption: Practical Tools for Today's Parents*. Indianapolis, Indiana: Perspectives Press, Inc., 2002. 157-158.

"Proverbs 18:1 New King James Version." *Bible Gateway*. Web. 26 Aug. 2012.

Schooler, Jayne E. and Thomas C. Atwood. *The Whole Life Adoption Book: Realistic Advice for Building a Healthy Adoptive Family*. Colorado Springs, CO: NavPress, 2008.

Smith, Darron T., Cardell K. Jacobson, and Brenda G. Juarez. *White Parents, Black Children: Experiencing Transracial Adoption*. Lanham, Maryland: Rowman and Littlefield Publishers, Inc., 2011.

Chapter 9:

Brodzinsky, David M., Marshall D. Schechter, and Robin Marantz Henig. *Being Adopted: The Lifelong Search for Self*. New York: Doubleday, 1992.

Bronson, Po and Ashley Merryman. "See Baby Discriminate." *The Daily Beast*. Web. 4 Sept. 2009.

James, Arleta. *Brothers and Sisters in Adoption: Helping Children Navigate Relationships When New Kids Join the Family*. Indianapolis, Indiana: Perspectives Press, 2009.

Johnston, Patricia Irwin. *Adoption is a Family Affair!: What Relatives and Friends Must Know*. Philadelphia: Jessica Kingsley Publishers, 2012.

Keefer, Betsy, and Jayne E. Schooler. *Telling the Truth to Your Adopted or Foster Child: Making Sense of the Past*. Westport, Connecticut: Bergin & Garvey, 2000.

Melina, Lois Ruskai and Sharon Kaplan Roszia. *The Open Adoption Experience*. New York: HarperPerennial, 1993.

O'Toole, Elisabeth. *In On It: What Adoptive Parents Would Like You To You Know About Adoption*. St. Paul, Minnesota: Fig Press, 2011. 45.

Pertman, Adam. *Adoption Nation: How the Adoption Revolution is Transforming Our Families — and America*. Boston, Mass.: Harvard Common Press, 2011. 117.

Schooler, Jayne E. and Thomas C. Atwood. *The Whole Life Adoption Book: Realistic Advice for Building a Healthy Adoptive Family*. Colorado Springs, CO: NavPress, 2008.

Simon, Rita J., and Rhonda M. Roorda. *In Their Own Voices: Transracial Adoptees Tell Their Stories*. New York: Columbia University Press, 2000.

Tatum, Beverly Daniel. *"Why Are All the Black Kids Sitting Together in the Cafeteria?": And Other Conversations About Race*. United States: Perseus Books Group, 1997.

Verrier, Nancy Newton. *The Primal Wound: Understanding the Adopted Child*. Baltimore, MD: Gateway Press, Inc., 1993.

Watkins, Mary and Susan Fisher. *Talking With Young Children About Adoption*. New Haven: Yale University Press, 1993.

Chapter 10:

Angelou, Maya. "31 Quotes on Siblings." *Psychology Today*. 13 Sept. 2011. Web. 1 Sept. 2012.

Crenshaw, Shirley. Personal Interview. 24 Jul. 2012

James, Arleta. *Brothers and Sisters in Adoption: Helping Children Navigate Relationships When New Kids Join the Family*. Indianapolis, Indiana: Perspectives Press, 2009.

Overstreet, Bonaro. "31 Quotes on Siblings." *Psychology Today*. 13 Sept. 2011. Web. 1 Sept. 2012.

Schooler, Jayne E. and Thomas C. Atwood. *The Whole Life Adoption Book: Realistic Advice for Building a Healthy Adoptive Family*. Colorado Springs, CO: NavPress, 2008.

Chapter 11:

Ashimolowo, Matthew. *What is Wrong With Being Black?: Celebrating Our Heritage, Confronting Our Challenges.* Shippensburg, PA: Destiny Image Publishers, Inc., 2007.

Gray, Deborah D. *Attaching in Adoption: Practical Tools for Today's Parents.* Indianapolis, Indiana: Perspectives Press, Inc., 2002.

James, Arleta. *Brothers and Sisters in Adoption: Helping Children Navigate Relationships When New Kids Join the Family.* Indianapolis, Indiana: Perspectives Press, 2009.

Johnston, Patricia Irwin. *Adoption is a Family Affair!: What Relatives and Friends Must Know.* Philadelphia: Jessica Kingsley Publishers, 2012.

Juneteenth: A World Wide Celebration. n.p., 2012. Web. 2 Sept. 2012.

Lincoln, Abraham. "Abraham Lincoln." *The Quotations Page.* 3 Sept. 2012. Web.

Schooler, Jayne E. and Thomas C. Atwood. *The Whole Life Adoption Book: Realistic Advice for Building a Healthy Adoptive Family.* Colorado Springs, CO: NavPress, 2008.

Socrates. "Socrates." The Quotations Page. 3 Sept. 2012. Web.

Tatum, Beverly Daniel. *"Why Are All the Black Kids Sitting Together in the Cafeteria?": And Other Conversations About Race.* United States: Perseus Books Group, 1997.

The Official Kwanzaa Website. Kwanzaa: A Celebration of Family, Community and Culture. n.p., 2012. Web. 2 Sept 2012.

Chapter 12:

DuBois, W.E.B. "W.E.B. DuBois." *African American Quotes.* 3 Sept. 2012. Web.

CPSIA information can be obtained at www.ICGtesting.com
Printed in the USA
LVOW10s1925200813

348821LV00021B/1122/P

9 781478 310860